D1570313

Garo Yepremian's Tales from the Dolphins

By
Garo Yepremian
and
Skip Clayton

Sports Publishing L.L.C.
www.sportspublishingllc.com

Interior photos courtesy of the Miami Dolphins, unless otherwise noted.

Director of production: Susan M. Moyer
Project manager: Jim Henehan
Dust jacket design: K. Jeffrey Higgerson & Joseph T. Brumleve
Acquisition editor: Scott Rauguth
Developmental editor: Stephanie Fuqua
Copy editor: Cindy McNew

ISBN: 1-58261-550-0

Printed in the United States of America

Sports Publishing L.L.C.
www.sportspublishingllc.com

Table of Contents

Garo Yepremian

To my wife, Maritza
The love of my life—

Thank You for believing in me
and standing by me
these thirty-one wonderful years.

Chapter 1

The Team

When I warmed up during the Super Bowl years, we averaged 80,000 fans a game. At least 20,000 were in the stadium before the game, and quite a few of them would gather behind the goal posts just to see me kick.

Kicking one from 55 or 58 yards away was new to the fans, so I would put on a show. They would cheer like it was the game itself. The fans got me up, but unfortunately at the end of the warmups, I always said to myself, "You are crazy. You went out there and made all of those field goals just to show off. Now you are dead tired." But the more tired and loose I was, the better I kicked the ball in the game. It never bothered me until I got older and had pulled hamstrings and groin muscles. Then I had to cut down.

If I had the wind with me, I would try 60-yard field goals. If I kicked against the wind, I wouldn't try anything longer then 50 yards. I made sure to kick against the wind to get an idea on how the wind was blowing. When I went out to kick against the wind, I reminded myself that I had made them in practice and to keep my confidence up.

My holder practiced with me in the beginning of the warmups, but if he was a quarterback, he had to leave, and I would get some young volunteers, usually a coach's son, to hold for me. After I practiced my field goals, I would do about 25 kickoffs.

I've been asked, "How does it feel to be booed in a game?" I tell people I don't know. I played in the NFL for 15 years and was never booed. I must be one of the lucky ones.

We are still a close-knit team today. There are hundreds of players in the Hall of Fame and thousands of athletes who played in the National Football League, but only 45 players went undefeated in one season. We are a family. We have reunions and our families and the coaching staff's families are there. Everybody was a big part of the family. It seems like yesterday when we were on the field.

Coach Shula takes as much pride in our undefeated season as anybody else. We wouldn't have had a perfect season without him leading us. He knows that without us he wouldn't be remembered as the coach of the only undefeated team. Shula always appreciated all his players and treated us right.

When my wife thinks about the deaths of Dorothy Shula and Judi Griese, tears come to her eyes. We feel the same sadness when we remember Bob Matheson and Wayne Moore, who have passed away.

When we played, the coaches and players often didn't see things the same way, but we do today. We are older. When we see each other, we knew we did something together that nobody else has since.

The Dolphins once had a big brawl with the Cardinals in St. Louis. Both benches cleared. It all started with Conrad Dobler, the craziest lineman ever. (He would bite guys' fingers or go for the knees.) He got out of hand, and next thing you know, the fights broke out. It took at least five minutes to clear the field. A couple of guys were fighting, but the rest were pushing and shoving. Some were trying to break it up.

The only people who stayed off the field were the coaches, Bob Griese, Larry Seiple, and myself. The fines were announced the next day. The only ones who weren't fined were the ones who stayed off the field.

Later Dobler was my teammate in New Orleans, and I got to know him. I thought he was quite a nice guy off the field. He had hundreds of great stories, and you didn't have to twist his arm to hear them. By then he was beat up and couldn't straighten his right leg because of all of the operations he had. He was in the locker room four hours before each game, lying down with hot pads underneath him and on top of him, and the trainer would work on him to loosen him up. The trainer thought Dobler would be in trouble if he didn't get treated every day.

Coach Shula wouldn't allow dirty play. He wanted every player to use every advantage he could get, as long as it wasn't dirty or against the rules.

Shula went by the rules. In the nine years I was with the Miami Dolphins, we were the least penalized team in football. He made sure that every player knew the rules and knew what was allowed. If somebody did something that was really against the rules, Shula would get all over that player.

Shula was on the rules committee, and he stood by his convictions. Those were the things that I admired about him.

A few times when we got back to the airport after a game, there was a major storm, and we couldn't take off. After a game, you want to get home, especially if the team lost, so storms were frustrating.

Other times, we left in great weather and ran into a storm halfway home. I always thought if lightening hit the plane, the team would be wiped out. I prayed, and players who didn't believe in God prayed too.

Our longest flight was to Seattle, but in my years in Miami, we only had to go there once. The food was great on the flights. On return flights home, we were handed six-packs of beer. I could only drink one. I would pass the rest to my card-playing friends. A cold sub was passed out prior to takeoff, and later we were given a choice of steak or chicken for a meal.

I was attempting a field goal against the Jets in Shea Stadium when the ball was snapped over my head. I went after it, and the outside rushing defensive back tried to pick up the ball. I kicked it out of his hands and out of bounds in front of the Jets bench. Johnny Ebersole of the Jets plowed me over, and they got the ball deep in their own end of the field. But we did prevent them from scoring a touchdown and went on to win the game.

While I was on the bus after the game, I had trouble breathing all of a sudden. I couldn't laugh, move or take a deep breath. I thought I was having a heart attack. I told one of my teammates what was happening, and he said that I must have cracked my ribs.

The next day the doctor verified that I had cracked two ribs. He told me to put some heat on it, and the following Sunday before our next game, the doctor gave me a shot in the area where I was hurting. I thought this was wonderful; no pain.

But after I kicked for 10 minutes during warmups, the pain was right back. I thought the doctor would give me another shot, but the trainer told me to take some aspirin and said the doctor could not give me any more shots. My kickoffs were short, and the papers wrote that I was losing it. They didn't know I was hurt. It cleared up after six months, but by then the season was over.

Years later I was playing in a golf tournament and saw John Ebersole. The first thing he said to me was, "Garo, how are your ribs?" So that was our joke every time we saw each other for the next three or four years. Once I went to Atlantic City for a golf tournament, and I saw Johnny at the cocktail party and his head was completely shaved. A lot of players were doing this at the time, and I thought that Johnny wanted to look cool. This looked like the perfect time for me to get back at him, so as my wife and I passed by I said, "Johnny, nice hairstyle. Nice." He told me he went through chemotherapy. I could have dug a hole and stayed in it, I felt so bad.

We wrote him a nice note and told him that we were praying for him and pulling for him to get better. Thank God he is doing well, and his cancer is in remission. He knew that I didn't know the situation about his cancer and that we were always joking. We are still great friends. I see him three to four times a year, and he still gets on me about my busted ribs. He is a councilman in Altoona, Pennsylvania.

When we went on the road, we practiced the day before the game in that team's stadium. There would always be kids sitting in the stands watching us work out. Every time I kicked a ball into the stands, the kids would throw the football back, except for the kids at Shea Stadium in New York. Any ball that got kicked in those stands, they grabbed it and were gone. They were the fastest kids that I ever saw. They went right out of the stadium with a $60 ball. Goodbye. After a while, we had to move to the open end of the stadium to avoid them.

If I was kicking against a team that had a great kicker, it brought the best out of me. A lot of kickers told me that they wanted to be at their best against me. In 1971, when Shula told us who was picked for the Pro Bowl, he said, "Jan Stenerud was selected as the kicker. Garo, you were robbed. You were supposed to be in that game. We can make up for it by winning the playoff game against the Chiefs in a couple of days."

We went to Kansas City and beat them in the longest game in football history. Stenerud missed a 32-yard field goal in regulation, and in overtime Nick Buoniconti blocked his attempt at a 45-yard field goal. I missed from 52 yards before I kicked the winning field goal from 37 yards out. To this day, Stenerud won't talk about the game. A lot of his teammates told me he still feels terrible about it. He was a great guy and sent me a nice telegram after the game congratulating me and wishing me the best in the Super Bowl. Stenerud is the only "pure" kicker to be inducted into the Pro Football Hall of Fame, but I was voted "Kicker of the Decade."

Exhibition games are meaningful because you want your team to improve and get ready for the season. Sometimes, coaches don't use all the personnel. What they do is use players to see what they can do in certain situations.

During those games, you work hard and learn all the plays. After that, you learn how to win. A lot of players from the draft came from teams that never won. They had to get acclimated to the players on the Dolphins who were used to winning championships.

In the 1972 exhibition season, we lost to Washington and beat them in the Super Bowl. The following year, we lost to Minnesota in the exhibition season and also beat them in the Super Bowl. When we played those teams in the Super Bowl, we didn't give those early losses a thought.

Jake Scott runs the ball down the sideline.

Defensive coach Bill Arnsparger left in 1976 to become the head coach of the New York Giants. Vince Costello was hired to take his place. His ways were different then Arnsparger's, which was normal. During the first training camp of the new season, the defense was working on new things when a big argument broke out. Costello called for a zone defense, and safety Jake Scott said that wasn't the way we did it when Arnsparger was here. Costello told him that he was here and it would be done his way, while Scott told him that they would do it the old way.

They had a big argument, and Shula jumped in and wanted to know what the yelling was all about. Scott told Shula, "I am not talking to you." He kept arguing with Costello.

A week later, we had our awards banquet for the previous season, and Coach Shula wanted everybody there. Scott said he wasn't coming, because he normally got paid to attend banquets. Shula told him that if he didn't come he would be fined, and Scott told him to go ahead. He still wasn't coming.

There were about 1,000 people at the banquet, and we had our wives with us. Shula was sitting at the head table, about three or four chairs down from owner Joe Robbie. They introduced us in numerical order according to our jersey numbers, and I was introduced first because I was number 1. After number 12, Bob Griese, was announced, Jake Scott, number 13, was next. They called his name, and he wasn't there.

Mercury Morris dodges a would-be tackler on his way to a big gain.

Robbie yelled at Shula, attacking him and asking him, "What kind of a coach are you? Can't you teach discipline to your players?" Shula made a dive for Robbie, and they had to be separated. They had a strained relationship for the next four or five years and would only talk when there was business to be discussed.

After the banquet, Scott was traded to Washington for Bryant Salter. He only stayed four weeks. Everybody said that was the worst trade that Shula ever made, and we were only 6-8 that year.

We opened the 1972 season in Kansas City's new Arrowhead Stadium. I kicked two field goals, from 47 and 15 yards, and we won the game, 20-10. Larry Csonka rushed for 118 yards. The streak was underway.

The next week, we played our home opener and beat Houston, 34-10. "Mercury" Morris rushed for 94 yards, Csonka ran for 79 yards and Jim Kiick picked up 55 yards. They all scored touchdowns.

Then we went to Minnesota to play the Vikings. It was freezing cold, and they were beating us 14-6. I had kicked two field goals, from 38 and 42 yards.

With only about four minutes left in the fourth quarter, we were on the 44-yard line, and it was fourth down. I figured Coach Shula would go for the first down and make it a shorter field goal or go for a touchdown. Shula said, "Field goal." He didn't ask if I could make it. He was very positive. (My previous longest field goal was 47 yards.)

Shula said, "Garo, it is a 51-yard field goal. Go and kick it." Well, if Shula had confidence in me, I might as well have confidence in myself.

On my way out to the field, I prayed, "God, don't let me embarrass myself. Give me guidance to hit the ball well." We lined up, and I kicked the ball. It was beautiful. It went through the goal posts to make the score 14-9 with three minutes to go.

I figured we would go for the on-side kick, but I was told to kick it deep. Everything Shula called was working because he was experienced and he was a genius.

The Vikings got the ball on the 21-yard line. Quarterback Fran Tarkenton was a little conservative and would often take some time off the clock by running the ball. They ran it twice, threw it once, and didn't get a first down. There were about two minutes left when we got the ball back on our own 41-yard line.

Griese brought us down the field, and we got to the three-yard line. Griese got the ball, scrambled to his right, and no one was there. Griese scrambled to his left and spotted Jim Mandich, our tight end, in the end zone. Griese threw the ball with 1:28 left on the clock, and we scored a touchdown.

The following week, we played the New York Jets in New York. We were ahead, 24-17, in the fourth quarter and there was a chance they could tie it. Fortunately, I kicked a 43-yard field goal with a minute and half to go. That put the game out of reach. We won, 27-17. Csonka rushed for 102 yards.

Our next two games were in the Orange Bowl. First, we beat San Diego, 24-10, but it was a costly victory. Bob Griese suffered a broken bone in his right ankle and didn't play again until the last game of the season against Baltimore. We thought that was it for the season, but we realized

Jim Mandich catches a pass for a big play.

we had a great quarterback on the bench, Earl Morrall, whom Shula had claimed off waivers the previous April when the Colts released him. He came in and won the next 10 games. Morrall was older, but he knew the game and was a leader. Coach Shula had a lot of confidence in him.

During the Chargers game, Morrall threw two touchdown passes. After we beat San Diego, 24-10, we defeated Buffalo, 24-23. I kicked a 54-yard field goal, my longest. Morris rushed for 106 yards, while our defense held O. J. Simpson to 45 yards.

After we beat Buffalo, two of our next three wins were shutouts over Baltimore (23-0) and New England, which was our most lopsided victory at 52-0. We were ahead 38-0 when Shula took out Morrall and put in our third-string quarterback, Jim Del Gaizo. He went in with instructions to keep the ball on the ground. Shula didn't want to roll up the score and embarrass the other coach and his team.

At that time, the quarterbacks called their own plays. Del Gaizo called a deep post and threw a 51-yard touchdown pass to Marlin Briscoe. Coach Shula went nuts and told him to keep the ball on the ground. We got the ball back again after they fumbled, and Del Gaizo threw a 38-yard touchdown pass to Briscoe. Shula went crazy. All Del Gaizo did was showcase himself for the rest of the league.

Next we topped the Jets, 28-24, but we trailed, 24-21, in the fourth quarter when Morris scored on a four-yard run. Our final touchdown was set up when Dick Anderson recovered a fumble. When we beat the Jets, we clinched the AFC east. There was no slowing down. We defeated the St. Louis Cardinals 31-10 as Anderson recovered a fumble and had an interception. Lloyd Mumphord returned an interception for a touchdown. Csonka rushed for 114 yards, and Morrall completed 12 of 19 for 210 yards.

Larry Csonka hammering his way through the line.

Our next two games were on the road. We beat New England 37-21 as Csonka went over 1,000 yards rushing for the season. Then we beat the New York Giants in Yankee Stadium 23-13 for our 13th straight win on a muddy day. I had to take my towel onto the field and wipe up the mud so I could get a good spot for the ball. I made three field goals from 37, 31 and 16 yards.

In our final regular season game, we beat Baltimore in the Orange Bowl, 16-0. I kicked field goals from 40, 50 and 35 yards. Griese came back and played part of the game, and Morris got to 1,000 yards rushing, which made the Dolphins the only team to have two players rush for 1,000 or more yards in the same season.

There was a lot of pressure on us when we went into the playoffs in 1972 because we were undefeated. We weren't saying we had three games to play. We thought only of the next game, taking it one at a time. We had to win the first against Cleveland and then relax for a day.

Cleveland was very tough and led us 14-13 in the fourth quarter. I kicked a 40-yard field goal in the first quarter and a 46-yard field goal in the fourth quarter. We scored late in the fourth on Kiick's eight-yard run to win it.

Next, we had to go to Pittsburgh and play the Steelers in Three Rivers Stadium. A week earlier, they had won their game over Oakland on a miracle catch (the Immaculate Reception) by Franco Harris at the end of the game. We had a tough time in Pittsburgh, and they were doing a better job. We were behind 7-0 in the second quarter, but fortunately Seiple got the ball to punt; then he looked and saw that nobody was there to guard him. Seiple tucked the ball under his arm and ran downfield for a big first down. That was the turning point in the game.

Morrall threw a nine-yard touchdown pass to Csonka. Griese came in for the second half and led us to two more touchdowns, and we won, 21-17, to go to the Super Bowl for the second straight year.

We went 17-0 that season, which is a great record. Now teams play 16 games in the regular season, so they have to go 19-0 to be undefeated. If a team starts out with ten or twelve wins and no losses, I like that, because it brings excitement back and people think of the 1972 Dolphins and the fact that we are the only undefeated football team in history.

If a team gets to 13-0 or 14-0, then we get nervous, thinking maybe that club can do it. We don't have anything against them, but we start worrying and talking about it when we see our old teammates. But as soon as that team loses and their winning streak ends, we breathe a sigh of relief.

Not that we wish anybody to do badly, of course. If some team does go undefeated, I will tip my hat to them and say, "Great. Now there are two undefeated teams." But until then, we can still say we were the best.

Earl Morrall

As a good example of how seriously we take the record, the Chicago Bears came to Miami in 1985 with a 12-0 record. Mike Ditka was their head coach, Buddy Ryan was their defensive coordinator, and they had a great defense. Jim McMahon was their quarterback, and they had a great runner, Walter Payton. They came into Miami with a head of steam for a Monday night game.

In the two previous games the Bears had shut out Dallas 44-0 and Atlanta 36-0. A lot of my teammates were on the sidelines during the game, and this made the 1985 Dolphins happy. They got excited and were focused. Coach Shula was still there, and he had the team fired up. He didn't want his record to go down the drain. He didn't need any phone calls, but I have a feeling a lot of the guys in Miami called anyway.

Shula prepared his team accordingly, especially for that game, which was one of the most important in his career. They played better than they had played all year and beat Chicago 38-24. The Bears won the rest of their games and finished 18-1. We took our hats off to the 1985 Dolphins who took care of business for the 1972 Dolphins.

Earl Morrall is a super human being. He worked very hard as a backup quarterback. He was my holder not only during games, but also during practice. After he worked out for two hours in practice, he would come over, get down on his knees and hold the ball while I practiced. If I wanted to do some extra kicking, he stayed and never complained. We had great timing, and Shula made sure that we had enough time to practice.

Shula also knew that games were often won or lost on an extra point, a field goal, a blocked punt, a punt return or a kickoff return. He knew that 33 percent of the game is special teams, and he appreciated those players.

If the Green Bay Packers, New York Giants or Chicago Bears had gone undefeated, they would have gotten more publicity and recognition then we did. In New York, they would have been naming streets after all the players. Miami was a small market then that didn't have baseball, basketball or ice hockey. All Miami had besides the Dolphins was the University of Miami, and they were an up-and-coming team that wasn't drawing big crowds.

When Shula got to Miami in 1970, our attendance went up from 34,687 in 1969 to 62,877. He brought in new players and excitement, which was a big thing. At first, games were social events. Then it started to become more serious, and they had to add seats in the Orange Bowl.

I had a great relationship with Shula and sat in on his meetings every day because I was a part of the team. At first, I thought, "What am I doing here? I don't need this. I am a kicker. I don't have to listen to all of this." Later on, I realized I learned a lot. He helped me to go against all odds and give a little extra. His strategy was "the winning edge"–to do something more than the other team, take it one step further.

After I retired, I did everything to the best of my ability and took it one step further. When I give motivational speeches to major companies, schools and colleges, I teach the same principles.

I am often asked what kind of an education I had. I tell them I left school when I was 15 and educated myself. I speak four languages: English, Armenian, Greek and Turkish. I came to this country in 1966 speaking broken English. I could understand, but I had trouble communicating. I had a very heavy accent and started working on it. Now people ask me if I can speak English. I amaze them when I tell them that I talk to major companies for an hour without a note in my hands.

Coach Shula would come into our meetings and talk for 30 minutes without a note in front of him. He knew what to say. He got right to the point and made people understand if they work hard, if they were decent and honest, sooner or later, they would persevere.

When we played Kansas City on Christmas Day in the 1971 playoffs, we thought we were a decent team, but we didn't think we were a super power. We went to Kansas City as the underdogs. The Chiefs had *the* offense of the '70s.

We felt we had a good chance of winning it, but we weren't sure of ourselves. Since the Dolphins came into the league in 1966, they were 0-6 against Kansas City, but that was before Shula got to Miami.

We won the longest game in the history of pro football, and we became believers in ourselves. That turned the whole thing around for us, from a team that was good enough to make the playoffs to a team that was good enough to win it all. That was also the downturn for the Chiefs. They never won anything after that, and it gave us confidence. We went on to play the Cowboys in Super Bowl VI.

Against Kansas City, we were tied 10-10 at the half. We fell behind 17-10 in the third quarter, and then we tied the game as Kiick scored on a one-yard run in the third quarter. The Chiefs went ahead 24-17 in the fourth quarter, but we came back and tied the game with 96 seconds left when Griese threw a five-yard touchdown pass to Marv Fleming. I kicked the winning field goal in the second over-time from 37 yards out, ending a kickers duel with Jan Stenerud.

We were a no-name team. We had discards from other teams, no big names and no superstars, but our offensive line started with Jim Langer, center, who was picked up from Cleveland. Bob Kuechenberg, left guard, played with the Chicago Owls in the Continental League. Wayne Moore, left tackle, was in San Francisco when we picked him up. Larry Little, our right guard, was let go from San Diego. Norm Evans, our right tackle, came from Houston in the 1966 expansion draft.

Our defensive line had Bill Stanfill, Bob Heinz, Kevin Reilly and Manny Fernandez. We had, at times, three line-men and four linebackers. We had the 5-3 defense because Bob Matheson, who was a linebacker, would double up as a defensive end.

Manny Fernandez is determined to tackle the ball carrier.

My weight had to be no more than 170 pounds. I could live with that, but if my weight went up to 168, I got nervous. Every Thursday morning, Carl Taseff would check our weight, and he kept a chart. If you were over, you were fined $25 per pound per day until you lost it.

I was never fined, but I came close in 1972 or 1973. I checked my weight at home, and I was three pounds over. I put on rubber pants and a rubber jacket and hopped into my Cadillac. It was 80 degrees. I kept the windows closed and the heater on full blast. It was a 28-mile ride to practice. I had 30 minutes to get there, but at the same time, I didn't want to be late for practice. Everybody who saw me had to be thinking I had my air conditioner on, but I looked like a red beet.

I got to the parking lot soaking wet. I went in and was three pounds under. After I was weighed, I started drinking water and orange juice. If they had weighed me 20 minutes later, I would have been four pounds over.

We had a backup offensive lineman around 1976 who ran on the kickoff team against the New York Jets. He was slow because there was water all over his waist. You could see the flab.

Two days later, they had a surprise weigh-in. He was 13 pounds overweight. Coach Shula said he wouldn't fine him that day because it was a surprise weigh-in, but he gave him until Thursday to lose that weight. If he was still over,

Miami Dolphins coach Don Shula poses with quarterbacks Earl Morrall and Bob Griese on Jan. 3, 1973 in Miami. (AP Photo/file/ Mark Foley)

Shula said he would be fined. Quarterback Don Strock started a pool to see how many pounds over he would be.

Everybody was there on Thursday to see what he weighed. He got on the scale and was a pound and a half under, so nobody won the pool. Strock had to give everybody their money back.

We had the advantage over visiting teams who weren't used to the Miami temperatures. Our players were in great shape, and we were used to the heat and the humidity. When teams from up north came down, they left temperatures in the 50s for temperatures still in the 90s. When that humidity kicked in, we would look at the other bench and see them huffing, puffing and using oxygen tanks. We knew then that we had won half the battle. In the second half, they would wilt away.

At the same time, we had problems playing in cold weather. We had success but not as much as we had at home. When we went to New England and it was freezing cold, we knew they had the upper hand.

The Oakland Raiders were our toughest opponents. They were bigger physically and had bigger name players. Owner Al Davis always went out and got the meanest players. We started off the 1973 season by beating San Francisco 21-13 to run our winning-streak to 18 games. The following week, Oakland beat us 12-7.

The following year in the opening round of the AFC Playoffs, they beat us in Oakland 28-26, after Ken Stabler threw an eight-yard touchdown pass to Clarence Davis with eight seconds left in the game.

Chapter 2

The Super Bowl

I t was a freezing cold day for the 1972 Super Bowl at Tulane Stadium. The Superdome was being built, but it wasn't ready. The fans were frozen, and we were frozen on the field, but at the same time the Dallas Cowboys were confident. They had the veterans who had been there. They lost the year before to the Baltimore Colts, 16-13, in the final five seconds when Jim O'Brien kicked the winning field goal. We were so excited about being there that we felt we weren't even in the game.

For two weeks prior to the game, you are immortalized in a way. You feel like you are Superman because all of a sudden everybody is paying attention to you. You go to a restaurant, and they treat you like you are a king.

Miami was a young team, and we were partying every day. I thought this was wonderful. We got to the game, and reality set in. We weren't prepared. The veteran team was hungry and ready. They had lost before and wanted to take revenge on somebody.

A magazine took pictures of the teams in T-shirts and shorts. They took one picture of the eleven starters on offense and one of the starters on defense, but the Miami offensive picture had twelve because I was included. Coach Shula said that I was as much a part of the offense as anybody else.

When Dallas beat us, 24-3, we had that empty feeling that comes from knowing that we worked hard to get somewhere and came out empty handed. We didn't want it to happen to us again. Of course, we won the next two Super Bowls. We were the fourth team to play for the first time against a team that had been to the Super Bowl before. All of the first-time teams lost.

Continuing the trend, when we went back the following year and beat Washington, they had never before been to the Super Bowl.

The final game for the 1972 season was Super Bowl VII, our 17th game. All we had to do was win the game, and we were in business. The Miami Dolphins would be the only undefeated team in the history of pro football.

A funny thing happened the day before, when we practiced at the Rose Bowl. I was throwing passes to Coach Shula's son David during practice, because a kicker doesn't do much on the sidelines. I was throwing the ball 35 yards, and I felt like I was a great quarterback.

We were excited when we got to the Los Angeles Coliseum the next day for the game, but I soon realized I was having problems kicking the ball. I couldn't get it up high enough. I was hitting line drives and wasn't getting that nice lift off the ball. The problem was the ground. The field conditions were great, but kickers need to have good traction for their plant foot. I am left-footed, and my right foot had to be planted so that I could bend my right knee and lift the ball up.

During practice, I tried the rubber soles that I had for artificial turf, and they didn't work. I had medium-size cleats that didn't work. I put higher cleats on my right foot and thought they might give me better traction. But I had the feeling there wasn't much of a give to the soft and hard spots. The ground must have been hard, because when I planted my foot in, it didn't dig in.

I was really worried about blocked kicks. But usually if you didn't do well in practice, things worked out in the game. I wasn't the type of a guy to go to the coach and tell him not to try any field goals because I was having a tough time.

Fortunately for me, all I had to do was try two extra points. It was a very boring game. The Redskins couldn't do anything, and we ran all over them. We had a comfortable 14-0 lead, or it seemed comfortable enough with about four minutes to go in the fourth quarter. I was called in to kick a 42-yard field goal. I thought, "This is perfect." All I had to do was make this field goal and the score would be 17-0.

The snap was perfect. Earl Morrall put the ball down. Perfect hold. So far, so good. I kicked the ball, and it was a line drive into the line. It bounced all over the place.

Well, a kicker is taught to take something that is a negative and turn it into a positive. I thought that if I picked it up and threw it downfield, I might hit one of my teammates and we might score a touchdown. I only had a second to think about this. After throwing the ball well the day before, I thought I was going to be fine.

Earl Morrall, who was also the holder, hands the ball off as quarterback.

As soon as I picked up the ball, I saw Bill Brundige coming towards me with smoke coming out of his ears and mouth. It was a scary situation, and I didn't have time to fool around. I had the ball in my right hand and couldn't adjust the laces. My right leg was forward, and I didn't have time to adjust to my left leg. I tried to cock my arm to throw it. The ball fell out of my hands and went straight up in the air.

Gravity didn't even help me. The ball was coming down towards me, and if I tried to bat it out of bounds, everything would be fine. I hit the ball with my hands. It went up again, and Mike Bass of the Redskins caught it and went down the sidelines 49 yards for a touchdown.

All of a sudden the score was 14-7 with three and a half minutes to play. Washington had a chance to tie it, and if they did all of our dreams were down the drain. I was dejected, scared and embarrassed. There were more than 90,000 people in the stands and millions watching on television. The only thing I could do was run to the sidelines to the end of the bench and try to avoid Coach Shula, who could look through you with his eyes. He must have realized I was headed over there, so he went after me and cut me off at the pass. He was in my face, looked straight at me and said, "You should have sat on that ball."

He didn't have much time to waste with me. He had to worry about our defense, which did hold them, and we won the game, 14-7. I could have hidden, but I didn't. I had to face the music.

I went straight to the locker room and to my locker. All the reporters came after me. They should have been writing about the perfect season, but instead they wanted to find out about the one negative we had all year. The best way out of this was to answer all of their questions. After all, we won the game. What else could they do to me?

I made some jokes about the pass. I said, "I will never throw another pass again." And then I paused and said, "Until the next Super Bowl." I didn't know we would back in the Super Bowl the next year.

We weren't favored to win that Super Bowl. We had won 16 straight games and were the underdogs. How could we be the underdogs? We got to the stadium, and George Allen, the Redskins coach, was on the sidelines with his team. They were dancing up and down. If you looked at the Dolphins on the sidelines, we weren't showing any emotion, but we were ready to pounce on them.

Billy Kilmer was the Redskins' quarterback. He was a great competitor, but we were all over him. As soon as the ball was snapped, Manny Fernandez (who had his greatest game) was in the backfield as the ball was handed off. Their running backs were getting their heads knocked off, and Kilmer was being tackled before he even took any steps back. We were hungry.

We never received the respect that we deserved for the 1972 perfect season. People said that we were lucky, and they still say that to this day. We had to prove that we had a great team the next year. We had a better team but lost two games. Our record was 15-2 the next year and 32-2 over two years. We proved that we were the dominant team at that time, even though we didn't have the superstars. It was special that we were the first American Football Conference team out of the American Football League to win two straight Super Bowls.

We had a better team in 1973, even though we lost two games. We were like a well-oiled machine.

After that game, I went back to the hotel in Long Beach. The wives stayed in separate hotels from the team, but my brother was with me, and later on the rest of my family joined me. Everybody wanted to go to the victory party at the Beverly Hilton in Beverly Hills, which was 45 minutes away. I didn't want to go, because I was embarrassed. My family said I had to go because the team going undefeated was the greatest thing that would ever happen to me. "Sooner or later, you have to go and face the people," they said. I went, but I wasn't happy being there.

After about 20 minutes, I started developing something that I never had before in my life. The whole left side of my body was in pain. The pain in my leg was excruciating. I couldn't stand up. I couldn't sit down. My brother carried me to the car and drove me back to Long Beach while the party went on.

I tried to figure out what to do to rid myself of the pain. Once I got back to the hotel, I filled the bathtub up with freezing cold water and buckets of ice. I sat in it for about five minutes. I don't know how I tolerated that freezing tub, but when I got out of it the pain was gone. I have never told this story before, and I never had the pain again.

It must have been something psychological that affected my brain, and it shut off my body.

When we came back to Miami, 20,000 people greeted us at the airport. They had signs that said, "Garo is still Number 1." I had done a lot of great things that year, and those signs made me feel better. After Coach Shula showed the trophy, the fans started chanting my name.

I was one of the few players who was asked to say a few words, and I didn't know what to say. Finally I said, "Thank you very much. I will never throw a pass again until the next Super Bowl." Shula's eyes lit up, but the crowd laughed and thought it was the funniest thing they ever heard, and they were chanting.

For the next two weeks, I avoided going out. One day, I opened up my mail and there was a letter from Coach Shula. He wrote, "Garo, I know you have been getting a lot of flak the past few weeks for the pass in the Super Bowl. I want you to forget that. We won the game, and we are the only undefeated team. Without you, we wouldn't have been undefeated. You will be getting a Super Bowl check in the mail. Enjoy it, and I will see you in training camp." That made me feel wonderful, and it changed my whole attitude.

I started going out. I became the target of random guys who had probably never thrown a ball in their lives and would be scared just to walk on a football field. And yet they were putting me down. They would ask, "How is your passing arm?" or "What kind of a pass was that?" with a four-letter word thrown in. I took it in stride. I said, "We had an independent group come over and take a survey on my passing. We went to the Superdome where there isn't any wind. I threw a three-yard pass this time. It went forward, end over end." People laughed, and it broke the ice. I still get these questions 30 years later.

There are some situations where other kickers missed a field goal and lost a Super Bowl game, and you never heard from them again. I felt bad for those guys. But at the same time, sometimes I feel bad for my family. I had more points then anybody in the '70s. I made 20 field goals in a row, a record at the time, and I was in the Pro Bowl twice. But people think I am famous because of the one pass I threw. They don't realize I kicked field goals against all odds.

I made 51- and 54-yard field goals when the game was on the line. I was always consistent. All of that is forgotten, and one of the reasons I am not in the Hall of Fame, but my shoes are, is because they still dwell on the one pass that I threw.

We were never invited to the White House after we won. We never had a parade. And the same thing happened the following year. (Although maybe we weren't invited to the White House because of the political climate during the Nixon years.)

Garo attempts to put one through the uprights.

That summer we came back to training camp, and I started kicking. About halfway through the drill, Coach Shula stopped us and told me to kick it low and have it blocked. He wanted me to dive on the football. I had never done this before in my life. I lined up, kicked the ball low, and it was blocked. The football bounced all over the place. I ran over to jump on it and twisted my ankle. When I got up, I was hurt. Shula said, "That is the end of that drill. We don't need any kicks blocked from now on. Kick it high enough so you won't have to dive on the ball." Everyone laughed.

I thought of throwing the ball in that drill, just for kicks and to rattle Shula, but I knew where the line was drawn. Shula and about 20 other players would have jumped on me. The temptation was there, but my mind said, "Forget it. Don't get killed today."

A lot of the players understood what happened, but there were always one or two who resented the fact that I made a joke out of it. I had to keep my sanity, and if I hadn't made a joke out of it, people would have picked on me more. It would have gotten to me, and my performance would have suffered. So I made jokes out of it.

When people interviewed me, before they could say anything, I would tell them that my passing was great. "In fact," I said, "I am the only kicker in the history of football to have a perfect record. I am the highest-rated quarterback in the history of football, one for one with a touchdown."

A lot of my teammates saw I was doing a lot of promotional work, doing commercials and making speeches at banquets. They resented it because they thought my talent was just talking about my pass. It wasn't. I was there because people felt I was funny. I was articulate and had something to say, and they wanted to hear it. Sometimes I would throw in the pass, but 99 percent of the time I didn't bring it up. I let other people bring it up.

Even though we won, I have to suffer the humiliation for the rest of my life, and my kids will suffer for it for the rest of their lives–when my kids introduce themselves, people say, "Your dad screwed up in the Super Bowl." That bothers me, but you take it in stride and make a joke out of it.

One time I was at the airport, and a guy pointed me out to his son and said, "Garo Yepremian. He played 15 years in the NFL. Kicker of the decade. He played in the longest game in the history of football, played in three Super Bowls and scored over 1,000 points. Great kicker." He turned his back and walked away.

That was definitely a change of pace.

We did have a play for a fake field goal, but it was for my holder, who was either a quarterback or a wide receiver. Coach Shula felt the holder would be the one to get the ball, and I would try to block somebody while he threw a pass or ran with it. The coaches didn't trust me with my hands, which were made of stone. I couldn't handle the ball.

When someone asks me "How is your passing arm?" I tell him, "I don't remember that." Then the guy says, "I remember it like it was yesterday," and his wife will usually say he has a great memory. I say, "Really? I will give him a test right now."

Now he will get nervous, but I tell him that everybody passes this test. My question is "Do you remember last year's Super Bowl?" He'll say, "Of course. It was New England and St. Louis." Then next my question is, "Do you remember the last pass Kurt Warner threw in the fourth quarter?" He'll say, "No, I don't." I say, "Thank you very much. You remember mine 30 years later, so it must have been special."

At the press conference before the 1974 Super Bowl, the media asked me about throwing another pass. I made a joke out of it, saying, " I'm not going to throw another pass. I will avoid it at any cost."

Nobody pressed me on the subject. We were going to play Minnesota, who lost to Kansas City four years before.

Carl Eller, the great defensive end of the Vikings, felt that Miami was destined to win that game because that was what all the media was predicting. And we did dominate that game.

I was worried when we went to the 1974 Super Bowl. I didn't want the same kind of a situation that I had the year before. I only had one attempt in the game for 28 yards, and I really concentrated. We won the game 24-7. I was relieved I had not messed up, and finally I could celebrate at the Super Bowl winner's party.

C oach Shula was carried off the field both times we won the Super Bowl, but that was the extent of the celebration. There was a lot of press in the locker room, and it wasn't like a baseball locker room where everybody sprays champagne all over, because the NFL didn't allow it then. We didn't throw Shula in the showers, and we weren't dumping buckets of Gatorade or something else all over the coaches like they do today.

I make up stories about the pass when I speak at banquets. Here's a typical story that I tell:

"A year before, we lost to the Dallas Cowboys in the Super Bowl, 24-3. We weren't doing well. There was an emergency phone on the sidelines, and it rang at halftime. Coach Shula picked it up as he walked off the field. President Nixon was calling, and he liked to suggest plays. Nixon said, 'Coach, you didn't do well in the first half. I would like to suggest the flea flicker pass, because I think you will score a touchdown.' In the second half, we tried the pass, and it backfired. Mel Renfro picked it off and ran it back for a touchdown. Coach Shula lost a lot of respect in President Nixon's play calling.

"The next year, we played the Washington Redskins. Coach Shula called me over and said I was in charge of the emergency phone. This was part of my responsibility. I didn't have much to do during the game, so Coach Shula said, 'If it rings, pick it up and say, "Hi, this is Garo Yepremian on the 40-yard line of the Los Angeles Coliseum. May I help you?"'

"Nobody called until there were four minutes left in the game. I picked up the phone and a young lady said, 'Mr. Yepremian, I have the president on the line. Could you hold?' I was excited. I had only been in this country six years. This was a big honor for me to be talking on the phone with the president of the United States, the highest power in the world.

"All of a sudden, a voice came on the other end and said, 'Garo, make no mistake about this.' I realized this was President Nixon. I said, 'Sir, it is a big honor for me to be on the phone with you. If only my family, fans and teammates knew about this. What can I do for you?' The president said, 'I need a favor.' I said, 'Certainly, whatever you like. Do you need an autograph or something?' He said, 'Look, there are four minutes left on the clock. I have a wager with Vice President Agnew that the point spread will be seven points. Can you help me?' I told him I couldn't do that to my teammates, fans and family.

"There was silence on the phone for about two minutes. I heard the sounds of papers being shuffled around in the background. President Nixon came back and said, 'Garo, I have checked on your papers that you have filed to be a citizen of the United States.' All of a sudden, I changed my tune. I said, 'Sir, don't worry.'

"Then Coach Shula called me over and told me to kick a 42-yard field goal. I could kick 42-yarders in my dreams. It was an easy chip shot.

"I started thinking how to do this. If I kicked it low enough, it would be blocked, and I would not be blamed if something happened. I kicked it low enough and the ball bounced everywhere. Earl Morrall, my holder, told me, 'Pick it up.' I said, 'Why don't you pick it up?' He informed me he was 38 years old and had five kids at home.

"I decided to pick up the ball and throw it, not realizing my hand was too small. Bill Brundige came towards me, and I tried to throw it, but the ball slipped out of my hand. Mike Bass picked it off and ran it back for a touchdown.

"To cut the story short, six months later I became a citizen."

That is the story I tell at banquets, and I also tell them that I have a high regard for the office of the president. It is just a joke, because President Nixon gave the Redskins a play before the Super Bowl that didn't work. That is why I tell this story.

Chapter 3

Coach Shula

During the 1972 season, Coach Shula encouraged us to take it one game at a time–don't look past the team that you are playing, because they might beat you. After the 10th game, I heard some of the offensive and defensive linemen talking in the locker room about how the pressure would be off if we lost a game. But if we lost one in the playoffs, our season would be over.

Coach Shula overheard this and at the next meeting he said, "I hear a lot of talk about winning or losing a game. We are here to win every week, and we can't take any team lightly. We have to win this week and forget about next week. What we have done in the last ten games is gone now." Right away, we were focused on winning the next game. All of a sudden, the players said they wanted to win that week. We were going to do it, and nobody was going to stop us.

When we were on the sidelines, Shula had everybody stay in a certain area. On his left side, he wanted his offense. He would have the quarterbacks closest to him, then the wide receivers, tight ends, running backs and lineman. On the right, the middle linebacker and the rest of the linebackers were closest to Shula, then the defensive backs and linemen.

I always stood close to the coaches, ready to go in. I was nosy and wanted to know what plays they were running, and I got more inside stories that way. I wanted to know why Shula was yelling at somebody when he came off the field. It was boring if you sat on the end of the bench.

Coach Shula always preached to us not to use our mouths but our brains. He said, "Never say anything to get the other team fired up." He would have somebody go to the city of our next opponent and get the newspapers and see if they made any comments about us. Then he would use those articles to get us fired up. Shula told us not to say anything bad about other teams because if we did, that would give them ammunition.

He was very well prepared. If we were playing a road game, Shula would check out what the weather conditions were for the week. We didn't have the Weather Channel then. Today, you can check it out on television. I played for six coaches, and Shula was the most prepared coach of them all.

We didn't think much about the fact that Shula would be the first coach to have 100 wins in 10 years until the reporters said that he had 95 wins. Winning 100 games was special for Coach Shula, but it was also special for the players. He was the man who made winners out of us. It meant that we were major contributors. Without us, he couldn't have had the wins. We felt very special. The 100th win was in New England, where we won 52-0. Shula got a game ball.

He set the record for the most wins (325) by any coach in 1993 at Veterans Stadium in Philadelphia. I was there with my wife and two sons, Garo Jr. and Azad, when he won the game. My sons and I went to the locker room and got a big hug from him. Dan Marino was on crutches but was nice enough to come over and say hello.

I spent some time with Shula the night before the game at the hotel. I took him a nice box of chocolates. Coach Shula was the same before this game as any other game. I couldn't spend any time with Shula or the players in the lobby. The players had to lock themselves in their rooms because there were so many people hanging around the lobby. I went to the team meeting and got a chance to meet Pete Stoyanovich, the Dolphins kicker.

We had to play two games against the New York Jets each year. This was the club that had beaten Shula in Super Bowl III when he coached Baltimore. When we played the Jets, he never brought up the subject of that Super Bowl loss, and we never talked about it either. We didn't want to dwell on things from the past. We knew he wanted to beat the Jets and had been very hurt when he lost to them.

The worst part was the way his players had been so confident, saying things like, "No sweat, coach," or "We have this one." Shula always told us that you can't take anybody lightly, that every team is a worthy opponent, and that on any given Sunday, any team can beat any other team. We were aware of that. We swept the Jets in 1970. In fact during my nine years with the Dolphins, we beat them 14 out of 18 times.

If an opposing player dropped a pass in front of our bench, Coach Shula never said anything bad to him. He might say something to the effect that he didn't expect him to drop that one. He never said anything like, "I would hate to be in your shoes when you go off the field to talk to your coach." He might make a joke out of it, unlike other coaches.

After Shula took over in Miami, he never stressed the fact that we had to beat the Colts more then any other team. All of the games were important. I remember when his son, Dave, played for Baltimore as a wide receiver and a return specialist. The press made a big deal out of it, saying "Don Shula returns to Baltimore to play against his son and the Colts." We won the game, though. David caught a couple of fair catches, but they never materialized into anything.

Shula was afraid of man-eating animals, but who isn't? Some guys got an alligator and taped up his mouth and put him in the shower. When Shula went to take a shower, he turned on the water, looked around and saw the alligator. He got out of the shower as quick as he could. Shula knew right away that Bill Stanfill and Manny Fernandez were the practical jokers.

Coach Shula was very organized. It amazed me that he knew what would happen for the next two hours, right to the second. He had it all preplanned. He would come to the team meeting, and everybody would be at attention. We sat down and listened. We knew he was in command, and Coach Shula knew how to get everybody's attention.

He would write a list of exercises to do on the blackboard: jogging, calisthenics, stretching, etc. He was involved in every part of the game, while some coaches were just involved with the offense or the defense. We had seven coaches counting Coach Shula. Carl Taseff was our running backs coach, and he also did special teams.

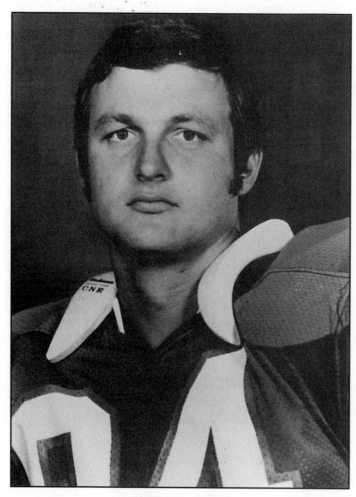

Bill Stanfill

Even though Bill Arnsparger was our defensive co-ordinator, there wasn't anything that Coach Shula didn't know. He knew every position as well as his coordinators. He worked very well with personalities and knew how to push buttons.

If he knew that somebody would perform better if he was put down, Coach Shula would do that. If he knew that somebody would perform better with some encouraging words during the week, he would do that. Coach Shula treated everybody fairly, but he demanded the utmost from everybody.

He was happy doing his job, and his motto was "The Winning Edge." It is inscribed in our Super Bowl ring. I remember when I first saw that motto in the dressing room, I thought they were doing a commercial for a shaving cream. Then I realized what Shula meant when he would say that we had to do everything the other team was doing but take it a step further. We had to be more prepared then the other team so that we would have the edge when we met them.

Shula wanted everybody to work hard. He was not only very well prepared with the starting lineup, but he brought in specific players to back up the starters in case someone got hurt. That was why he was so successful.

Coach Shula had us practice and practice, and he loved repetition. He figured the more you repeat things, the more you will remember them. The more you do things right in practice, the more things will go right in the game. Coach

Shula was competitive and a lot of people didn't like it, because when we went in to watch the practice films, he would take every play forward and backwards several times. After a while, you would get hypnotized and fall asleep.

It took me nine years of sitting in those meeting rooms to perfect the art of sleeping with one eye open and the other closed. I used to sit to the left of Coach Shula. If he turned to the left, he would see my right eye open, and he knew I was awake. As soon as I got this down, I was let go by Miami.

It also got warm in those rooms when we were watching film. The next thing you knew, you were asleep and snoring. If you did that, you got caught sleeping.

The one thing Coach Shula hated most was when he had about 20 players watching the offensive film and the room started to stink. There were always a few people who had gas. He hated the fact that grown people would make those noiseless bombs in public and stink up the whole place. It got so bad one time that he said, "Turn the light on. I am not going to take this. The coaching staff is not going to take this. If you guys are going to continue with all this gas, we will lock you in the room and the coaches and I are walking out."

When our meetings began, everybody was in one room. Coach Shula would tell us what we were going to do. After that, he would give us a pep talk and say, "You worked hard yesterday, but you should work harder today and do a better job. The next game is against a good team and we have to win this one." After that, we would break into groups based on positions.

Usually, I went to the meetings with the quarterbacks, running backs and receivers. I didn't have to be in there, but I felt I was more a part of the team if I was at the meeting, and my teammates would take me in because I was involved.

That was great. With Coach Shula, every part of the team was very important. Because I went to the team meetings, I learned about all of the aspects of the game, much more than I would have otherwise.

Today, I see Coach Shula at golf tournaments. I played in a tournament in Fort Lauderdale, Florida in 1999. He was talking to some people, and Nick Buoniconti, our team captain, was with me. We went to talk to Shula. He introduced me to the other people and said, "Here is my quarterback of the perfect season." Everybody laughed.

I said, "Look, Coach, after all of these years, I never thanked you for something." Shula asked, "What was that?"

"I was down in the dumps when I threw that pass, and you wrote me a wonderful letter," I said.

He didn't remember the letter, so I told him that he wrote me saying to forget what happened in the Super Bowl, that I was great part of the perfect team who should enjoy the $15,000 winner's check and the off season. That made me feel wonderful. He said, "I didn't write that letter. That must have been Dorothy." Everybody started laughing, because he took it as a joke. But his signature was there.

oach Shula has a great sense of humor, and he was always good to me during my playing career. He stood up for me many times. If I had a bad day, he was always there for me. He would get up in front of the team and say, "Garo has always done a lot of good things for the team. He had a tough week last week. We have confidence in Garo. He will do the job." The following week, I wouldn't miss any field goals. He definitely knows how to treat people.

Chapter 4

The Game

When I was kicking a field goal that could decide a game, opposing coaches took time-outs just to get me rattled. This could be nerve-wracking for a young kicker, but once you got some experience, it worked to your advantage. Personally, I was able to relax, check the angle and make sure my footing was right. But some coaches believed that when they took a time-out it bothered a kicker and gave him something else to worry about. Of course, if it is a cold day, the kicker does get cold standing around, and that could bother him.

When I kicked the winning field goal to beat Kansas City in the longest game, the Chiefs didn't call a time-out, and Hank Stram, the Chiefs' coach, wondered for many years if he had made the right choice. A couple of years ago, I was playing in a golf tournament with Stram, and he said to me, "Garo, I didn't take a time-out when you went out to kick." I told him, "You did the right thing. I would have been more comfortable if you had called a time-out." He said, "I knew I did the right thing."

When I kicked, the only person I talked to was my holder. He would encourage me, give me ideas about how the ground was and how the wind was blowing. He told me, "Don't let the other team rattle you. Just take your time, relax and do it like you did it in practice." It was to my advantage to have a good holder, because he knew all of the secrets.

The other team always tried to rattle me. They would yell and scream profanity at me; they would talk about my family and mention my sister. That bothered some kickers, but it didn't bother me. I didn't have a sister.

After I kicked a field goal, I never yelled back. I turned around and got ready to kick off. I did jump up and down a couple of times, but that was only if it was a game-winning kick in the playoffs. It was a little jump, because I couldn't jump very high anyway.

I thought Jan Stenerud (Kansas City), Roy Gerela (Pittsburgh), Toni Fritsch (Dallas), Horst Muhlmann (Cincinnati), John Smith (New England), Bobby Howfield (New York Jets) and Nick Mike-Mayer

(Buffalo) were the best kickers that I played against. Tom Dempsey, who booted a 63-yard field goal for New Orleans, was also a strong kicker. I give Dempsey credit for that kick, but he wasn't consistent.

I used to watch the other kickers to see if they got a good snap and a good hold. Everybody blames the kicker if he misses. There are times when it isn't his fault. Was the snap good? Was the hold good? Were the laces faced properly? If I got a bad snap or hold, I had about one-tenth of a second to make the adjustment on the kick. It takes 1.2 to 1.3 seconds from the snap to the kick. That isn't much time.

If I kicked a long field goal, I had to stand there and watch to make sure it went far enough. If it was 30 yards or less and I kicked it perfectly, I could turn away and listen to the crowd. In the longest game against the Chiefs, I kicked a 37-yard field goal in the second overtime. I knew it was good the minute it left my foot, before anybody realized it was. I raised my arms up and ran off the field with my back to the goal posts. When I didn't hear anybody cheering, I turned around and watched the ball go through the goal posts. Then I realized I was in enemy territory. They would have cheered only if I missed the kick.

On my way out to kick, I would say a little prayer, "God, let me be at my best. Don't let me let my teammates down." Then I would remind myself to keep my eye on the ball and follow through. When I headed onto the field, people were screaming, but when I lined up for a kick, there was complete silence. The holder always asked me, "Are you ready?"

I could see the center snap the ball out of the corner of my eye. I would start to make my move before the holder caught the ball. As he caught the ball, I was right there. The timing had to be perfect. If the kick was good, I would hear the fans scream. If I missed the field goal, I would walk off the field with my head down.

Kicking was one of the easiest jobs I ever had. I would have kicked for the rest of my life, if it were possible.

I liked to watch running backs, quarterbacks, receivers and linebackers. Gale Sayers was great, and some other good running backs were Floyd Little, Eric Dickerson and O. J. Simpson in his prime.

I thought Johnny Unitas was the greatest quarterback I saw. Joe Namath, Terry Bradshaw and Roger Staubach were also great. Then one day after I retired, I went to the Miami Dolphins' practice and saw Dan Marino play. I told my wife that I had just seen the greatest quarterback ever. She reminded me that it was only practice and the preseason, but I persisted. Marino was unbelievable.

Bob Griese was a great quarterback. He didn't have the tools that Marino had, but Griese had brains. He studied defenses and knew where to attack the weak areas. Griese didn't have the strongest arm, but he always got the ball there and got the job done.

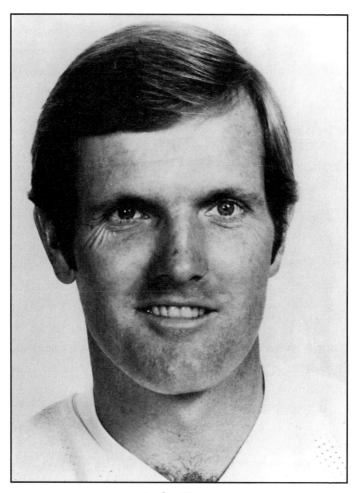

Bob Griese

Paul Warfield was the best receiver I ever saw. Nobody could touch him when he was in his prime. I never saw him drop a ball. Lynn Swann and Lance Alworth were two other great receivers, and Jerry Rice is the best now.

Jack Lambert, Willie Lanier, Nick Buoniconti, Dick Butkus and Ray Nitschke were five great middle linebackers. Two of the greatest outside linebackers were Ted Hendricks and Lawrence Taylor.

George Allen was a great coach. He was always well prepared, even going so far as to learning the wind pattern at the stadiums and when the sun would be at a certain angle so that he would know what goal posts to defend if he had a choice. Chuck Noll was a great coach. His Pittsburgh Steelers won four Super Bowls in the '70s. Shula was always aware of each week's opposing coach and his tendencies.

After games, I usually talked to the other kicker or a former teammate. O. J. Simpson of the Buffalo Bills, who was a superstar at the time, always came

Paul Warfield

over before and after the game to talk with me. He would put his arm around my shoulder and say hello.

I would always talk to Toni Fritsch, and he always said, "You and I are the best kickers, because we were great soccer players before we played football. These other guys don't know what they are doing. They don't have any technique, and they watch and steal from us." He was a funny guy and a good kicker.

One official, Armen Terzian, was very funny. Like me, he is Armenian. We were playing the Colts in Baltimore in 1973, and I was getting ready to kick off. Brian Herosian was returning kickoffs for the Colts, and he is also Armenian.

When the officials came out, they started counting the players on the field. Terzian looked at me and counted in Armenian. Then he said, "There are three of us on the field." I told him, "Today, the football stadium; tomorrow, the world." We started laughing, and the rest of the players wondered what was so funny.

When he made a call that Shula didn't agree with, Shula would yell "Armen, Armen, what are you doing to me?" to get his attention. Terzian would suddenly lose his hearing. He wouldn't turn back, because if he did, he would hear a lot more. The only time Terzian would talk to the coaches was when he couldn't avoid it.

The first time I walked into the Orange Bowl, I thought I was in heaven. The Detroit Lions played football in Tiger Stadium, which is a baseball field, and we played right on the diamond. We didn't have practice facilities, so we had to practice there. It was freezing cold, and the field was muddy. Half of the field (the infield) was covered with a tarp, so the whole team practiced on half a field. Today, every stadium is like heaven. All the NFL teams have great practice facilities and great stadiums.

My first impression of Miami was warmth, palm trees and swimming pools. The atmosphere was great. I said, "God has been good to me. I could still be in Detroit."

Except for my attempt at the Super Bowl, I never got a chance to pass or run the ball. I did recover a fumble, but I wasn't able to go anywhere with it. The ball was snapped over my head, and two guys were coming from the outside. I put the ball under my arm, and I couldn't believe how well I had that thing tucked in. One fumble recovery, no yards.

We played fourteen regular season games and six exhibition games. When the NFL went to a sixteen-game schedule, they cut back to four exhibition games. Six exhibition games were a bit too much. A lot of the players had their careers ended by injuries during exhibition games. Thank God they cut it down to four.

Today the hash marks are located at 70 feet, nine inches, but when I came in to the league, the hash marks were further out. They moved them closer to the center of the field in 1972, and it helped me a lot. The closer it was to the center of the field, the better it was for a kicker, because the angles weren't as severe. Prior to the hash marks being moved in, if you were kicking a short field goal, you had a severe angle.

Jan Stenerud of Kansas City and I kicked the ball over the goal posts on kickoffs consistently, so the NFL decided to move the goal posts back 10 yards to the end of the end zone and move the kickoffs from the 40-yard line to the 35. Later on, they moved the kickoffs to the present-day 30-yard line location. These were major moves to make the kickoffs more exciting and the extra points less automatic.

Prior to the start of the season, league officials would meet with the teams to go over the rules of wearing the uniform properly. Our socks had to be up. If we used white tape on black shoes, the officials said that we had to paint the tape black. The security office would talk to us about staying out of restaurants and clubs that had gamblers. Of course, we didn't know who the gamblers were. Nobody wore a tattoo on their head telling us they were gamblers. But they were trying to help us get through the year without trouble.

My first year in Miami, I made $13,000. They told me they would give me a 10 percent raise for the following year. There was no negotiating. It was take it or leave it. There wasn't any free agency, so we were stuck with what was offered. I signed for $14,300. I had a great year and led the league in scoring and percentage and was offered $17,000. Unlike today, we didn't get bonuses and long-term deals.

When people come to work on my house today and hear I'm a former player, they try to raise the price. I tell them, "I was making gas money and less than a postal worker when I played. Today, teachers get $40,000 and some of the players are in the millions. It is a major difference." That was how we played. I am not complaining. Football made me who I am and gave me a lot of great things, and I can't complain about that.

Lions coach Joe Schmidt said that soccer-style kickers wouldn't make it. It is just a fad. But people didn't realize that soccer-style kicking was the real thing.

Those players kick farther and more accurately. The kicking was different then. We used to play on fields that didn't have any grass. There were open-end stadiums with the wind blowing all over the place. We played in rain and snow, which they still do today, but most of the cities didn't have domed stadiums like they have today. If I were playing now, I would be kicking 90 percent. You can't compare kickers now to when I kicked.

I loved the Orange Bowl. The people were right next to you. The noise was unbelievable. We had sellouts for years. It wasn't the best stadium as far as the facilities went. Our locker room didn't even have lockers; all we had were benches with hangers, but the visiting locker room was worse. And there was always a swirling wind in the Orange Bowl, but once I knew what was happening, I was okay.

Shea Stadium in New York was a tough stadium to kick in, because the wind was always swirling, especially towards the open end of the stadium. Once I aimed the ball 20 yards outside the left goal post. The kick had a slight hook, and the wind was blowing left to right. The ball went straight up and started tailing to the right. It hit the right goal post and bounced back. That field also wasn't covered much, but when it was and they pulled the cover off, the dirt and grass would come off in chunks. There wasn't any traction.

Baltimore's Memorial Stadium was muddy and had a hard surface. It was a miserable field. Memorial Stadium and Shea Stadium were open-end stadiums. I always hoped we could score touchdowns and get out of there. I don't know why, but I had good luck and some of my best days there.

In New England, it was always cold and windy. We had a day where I was barely able to kick a 21-yard field goal, and our punter averaged that. Another bad stadium was Minnesota's Municipal Stadium. I kicked there in 1972. I missed three field goals in a game there in 1971. We ended up in a tie game—10-10. It was all over the papers that I had a bad day. Coach Shula said that he still had faith in me and that I would do great things for the team. The next week, I made five goals against Buffalo.

San Francisco had two stadiums that were tough to play in. First were the games in Kezar Stadium, before they moved to Candlestick Park. The stadium was below sea level, and it was always cold. It might be summer, and it was still cold.

The 1974 Pro Bowl was played in Kansas City on a frozen field. Maritza was home having trouble with a pregnancy, and she was going to have to stay in bed for the next couple of months. I didn't want to go to the Pro Bowl, but Coach Shula and Maritza made me go, because they both felt I was cheated out of it the year before. When I was assured that she would be taken care of, I left.

We couldn't practice in Kansas City because the weather was bad. They sent us to San Diego, and we practiced from Monday to Friday before flying to Kansas City on Saturday. I kicked my first field goal from 16 yards in the first quarter. When I kicked my second field goal from 37 yards out in the second quarter, I was watching the ball when Mel Renfro dove in to try and block it on the icy field. He skidded and hit me in the knee. My ankle and knee buckled. I was in excruciating pain and thought I had torn everything inside my leg.

They came to carry me off the field, but I knew I had to kick off. Ray Guy of the Raiders, who could kick off and punt, refused to kick off because he said that he was voted to the Pro Bowl just to punt. That was teamwork?

So I kicked off, but it wasn't a good one. I came to the sidelines, and they put me on ice. The ice came off in the third quarter, and I would go over and heat up my leg on the heaters so that I could kick. I was in such pain, but I thought I might not get another opportunity, so I wanted to make every opportunity count. I kicked a 27-yarder in the third quarter and a 41-yarder in the fourth, giving me four total field goals.

With 28 seconds left in the game, we were losing 13-12. I went in and attempted a 42-yard field goal. I knew my leg was gone, and I thought, "Just concentrate and do as well as you can." It went right through the goal posts.

The winners each got $2,000, and each member of the losing team got $1,500. The special teams coach gave me the biggest hug in the world, and he whispered in my ear, "My son will go to college for one more year." As I went off the field to the training room, there wasn't any doctor.

Jim Langer at center was the rock in the middle of the Dolphin offensive line.

Nick Buoniconti sheds a block on his way to the running back.

Bob Griese, Paul Warfield, Jim Langer, Nick Buoniconti and I flew back to Miami together. There was a drunk guy on the plane who looked at me and was acting like a wise guy and said, "Yeah, you were hurting. Five field goals, great acting. Ha ha ha." All of a sudden, Buoniconti came up behind him, grabbed him by the neck and squeezed him so hard that I thought his eyes were going to come out. Nick said to him, "Good acting? He almost tore out his knee and ankle and played through pain. Shut up and sit there." For the next 90 minutes, the guy just sat quietly.

When I got back, Coach Shula had a doctor waiting for me at the hospital. The doctor put me in a cast from hip to toe. For the first two days, I could take it, but then I started itching. After three days, I went to my parents' house and got a chisel and a hammer. Although my wife and mother protested, I started to cut off the cast. After I got halfway, I realized I couldn't cut anymore because I couldn't reach past my calf.

My brother helped me cut off the rest. Then I went to the drug store, got a knee brace, put it on, got in the pool and worked it out. Two weeks later, I won an NFL kicking contest.

Chapter 5

Training Camp

When we went out in the morning for training camp, the heat was always bad. We could only wonder how much hotter it would be in the afternoon. My first year with the Dolphins, we had four workouts a day. We started training camp late because of the strike. This was Coach Shula's first year coaching the Dolphins so we had a new system.

The first practice was at 7:30 a.m. in shorts and T-shirts, and it was already hot. That lasted an hour. After breakfast, there was a meeting. The 10 a.m. practice would be hotter. That lasted until 11:30. We wore shorts, shoulder pads, jerseys and helmets and thought Shula was going to kill the team–that he was crazy for overworking us. I thought we would be dead tired when the season began and wouldn't win a game.

There were a lot of people moaning and groaning the first week. Some of the players complained to the captains of our team. They went to Shula, but he told them that he had a new program. In order for us to get that winning edge over the other teams, we had to do more work then they did. When we started winning some exhibition games and saw that we were ahead of the other teams in conditioning, we followed his lead. After all, the Dolphins came into the league in 1966, and in the first four years, they had never won more than four games in a 14-game season. Once everybody started to realize that we were getting in great shape, we became believers.

The second morning workout was less difficult. It was a walk-through, but Shula didn't make it just a simple walk-through; we were running plays.

After lunch, we had a break. I went back to the room, and my roommate, linebacker Doug Swift, would always put on the television and watch a soap opera. I always complained to him, and he would laugh his head off at me. I couldn't take a nap because of the distraction, and I still can't take a nap today.

After Doug watched his soap opera, we would have meetings at 2 p.m., followed by an afternoon workout in full pads. If you didn't go out and practice in the heat, you weren't going to have a job. This was the hottest part of the day.

After dinner, we had another walk-through in shorts, followed by a meeting. We took four showers a day and were the cleanest guys in the whole world. The water department's best customers were the Dolphins.

In the years after, Shula had just two workouts a day in training camp because everybody knew the system, and the players were coming back. We only had extra workouts if we had a short week and had to play on Thursday night or Monday night.

Doug Swift was the first guy that said juice was great for you. He had a juicer that made carrot juice, and he would go to the market and find organic stuff. We would get a bushel of oranges and a bushel of carrots and bring them to our room. He made the juice every day. We had orange peels everywhere, and the next thing you know, our room was full of fruit flies. Of course in Florida, once in a while you get a roach here or there, regardless of how clean you are.

In the meantime, other players heard about Doug's juice. They stood in line to get a taste. By mistake one day, one of the reporters came and saw us, and he talked to me about the environment at camp because he'd heard about the guys who were coming and getting this juice. I opened my big mouth and said, "It's wonderful, and my teammates appreciate us, but they don't know I'm living in hell here." He asked what I meant, and I told him that when I wake up, I see a roach here, a roach there and a dozen fruit flies.

He then wrote that the Dolphins camp was infested with all kinds of insects. Well, Coach Shula went to church every morning at 5:30 a.m. and when he came back, he read the paper. During the next day's meeting, I was sitting in the front and coach hadn't taken his eyes off me. He said, "Some people, I won't name names, have the gall to say that we are staying in a training camp full of roaches and insects that are everywhere." I was chewed out that morning.

We made the rookies sing their alma mater for their first training camp. Ninety-five percent of them didn't know it. They would start singing the words, but before you knew it, they were humming it. Even then, they were off-key and didn't know the song that well.

The players who were bothered the most by the singing were the high draft choices. We used to call them "bonus babies." They came to camp and thought that they were "Mr. All-American" or "God's gift to the world." I remember one player who wouldn't sing. We tried everything, and finally the veterans picked him up and threw him in the lake. After that, he was mild-mannered.

Some rookies were arrogant, and some were nervous. In the beginning, they were doubtful, but once they got on the field and felt they would make it, their voices got stronger.

We didn't haze the rookies as much as the Detroit players did. We were more focused on winning.

There were guys who would slip out of training camp, but they were sneaking home to stay with their wives. They would park their cars outside the fence, close to their rooms, and figure out a way to get to their cars. As soon as the coaches checked their room, they would wait about 15 minutes and sneak out. When they came back, they went straight to breakfast. Roommates would take care of the room and make it look like both players were in there. That was the kind of team we had.

My wife Maritza would come by every afternoon at about 4 p.m. when practice ended. She would bring the boys, and I sat and played with them for a half-hour or an hour. At least I got to see the family.

Our house was about 25 miles away, but it took them 45 minutes to get to training camp because of the traffic. She did this for eight seasons. That was what made us a family, and the family came first. It was important to Maritza for everybody to be together.

Once, Coach Shula wanted me to practice blocking and tackling. For 10 minutes every day, I had to hit the blocking dummy. Each time I hit the dummy, my shoulder—which had been previously injured—was killing me. I went to the trainer's room after practice and said that my shoulder was hurting and I needed some kind of treatment. The trainer said, "Get out of here. You don't need any treatment. All you do is kick. We have more important things to do."

No one did anything for my shoulder. Since I retired, I have had three shoulder operations on my right shoulder and one on the left. That was life in the NFL then. I played 15 years and never missed a game or a practice. If you did, your job was in jeopardy, especially at my position. All they had to do was bring in another kicker and tell him to kick the ball through the goal posts.

I wasn't like a quarterback who had to learn the system. I was just a tire on the car. You change the tire with another tire. The quarterback is the transmission. It was easy to change the kicker.

So my wife was my trainer. She gave me ice packs, wrapped up my leg, gave me a heating pad for my lower back and massaged my knee or ankle or whatever was bothering me to get me ready for the next day. I didn't want the trainer to know I was hurting, because the next thing you know, Coach Shula hears about it, brings in another kicker, and you are out of a job.

I had confidence when I lined up. I didn't have a kicking coach, but I knew what I was doing. I knew how much I needed to kick. Sometimes if there were three or four thousand people watching us in training camp, I would put on a show.

A month before training camp, I always started to run in the stifling heat of South Florida. I ran for about 10 to 12 minutes and came back with my veins popping out. One day, I almost passed out in my living room. I must have overdone it, but I had to get in shape.

Jim Kiick

The only reason I got in shape was because the toughest day of training camp was the first one. First they checked our weight, and then we did our strength testing. They recorded those things to see if we were stronger then the year before. Next, we went out on the field and did calisthenics and some workouts.

Then Coach Shula made every player run six laps around two football fields in 12 minutes. It was usually around 98 degrees with 98 percent humidity. They had a coach on every corner with a stopwatch to make sure we were running. When we ran without the coaches around, it was easy.

Those two fields were side by side. After you ran two laps, you were completely soaked, and with the sun beating on your neck you were thinking, "I have to quit. I am going to die." Then something inside said, "You can't quit, because if you do, you have to run it again tomorrow. If not tomorrow, then the day after." Once we ran it, we were finished. During nine years at Miami, I made it every time. That was the challenge Shula gave us, and I was more worried about that than the competition.

"Mercury" Morris could run like the wind if it was a short-distance run. After three or four laps, he would throw up.

On the second day of camp, only the trainer would be there to see you run. Sometimes, I think the trainer cut corners to help some of the guys that had trouble running. You can overdue it and hurt yourself.

Larry Csonka and Jim Kiick were our two most outgoing personalities. We called them Butch and The Sundance Kid. One day they were running laps, and both stopped and started walking after three laps. Shula was at the opposite end of the field, and he yelled at them and told them to run. They didn't pay any attention to him. Shula ran the length of the field and went up to them, and they started to run again.

They go to the other end of the field and stopped again, so Shula had to run back the length of the field to get them started. They were both tired and wanted to walk, because they had gone too fast on their first couple of laps.

They eventually made their six laps, and Shula was in good enough shape to keep up with them.

At the end of each practice during training week, we did a drill called "gassers." We had to run from sideline to sideline twice in 30 seconds, stop, rest for 30 seconds, run it again, stop, rest for 30 seconds and then run it a third and final time. The kickers ran it in the same group as Shula and the quarterbacks. We did it twice a week during the season, and coach stayed in great shape.

Chapter 6

Funny Stuff

We had television's star dolphin, Flipper, in a tank in the end zone at the Orange Bowl because parents would bring their kids to the game, and they could see him. When I saw the tank, I asked what was done with the balls if they went in to the tank? Well, that was the best part. If a ball went in to the tank, Flipper flipped it out. I thought this was perfect. The team wasn't winning prior to 1970, but Flipper put on a show.

My goal was to not only kick the ball through the goal posts, but also kick it into the tank so that Flipper could pick it up, flip it out of there and get the people cheering. As soon as the ball went in to the tank, the fans cheered. Kids looked forward to this.

The pool was about 30 yards behind the goal posts. When I warmed up before the game, I kicked used balls, and no one cared too much about those going in the tank. But during the game, I started kicking into the tank. We scored more points, giving me the opportunity to kick more balls in there, and owner Joe Robbie didn't like it because the ball was ruined once it went in to the water.

He soon complained that I kicked too many into the pool and cost him money, and he asked people to tell me not to kick the ball into the tank. I still aimed for it, so Robbie put a net behind the goal posts. We were the first NFL team to put up the nets, and before long, all the other teams did it.

So I had a new goal after the nets went up–kick it through the goal posts but over the net. I did that a few times. The players loved it when I put the ball into the tank. They got excited about it, because they never had a kicker who was consistent. They knew good things would happen.

Today, when a guy does something special, he keeps the ball. He takes it over to the sideline, puts it in a bag and marks it so it doesn't get lost. We didn't have that luxury. We used to present only one game ball after each game. Coach Shula and the five team captains presented them. I have a dozen, including the one where I kicked the winning field goal in the longest game and the one where I kicked six field goals in one game with the Detroit Lions. I never saw the one that Mike Bass used to score the touchdown in the Super Bowl. These days the home team has to provide 36 new balls for outdoor games and 24 for indoor games.

I had a radio show on WIOD in Miami every Saturday night in the off season. Larry King had a show on the station at the time. He was great at interviewing people, and I really admired him. I always thought he was the greatest at interviewing people. My show lasted two seasons. We did an hour the first year (1971) and two hours the second year, except during the football season. It was difficult to have a show, because football was the only sporting event in Miami. Maritza was the producer, and she screened all the phone calls.

One time, I had my two barbers on the show, because they were big soccer fans and the World Cup was coming up. For 20 minutes before the show, they were talking up a storm about the whole tournament. The red light went on, and the show started. I mentioned my guests and introduced them, but they were speechless. I thought they were going to pass out. They answered every question with a yes or no, so I knew I was in for a long night.

I started to work for another radio station at the same time and did a daily five-minute show in 1972. I would tape the five minutes ahead of time and send it in over the telephone. We went to Europe for 30 days, and I taped 30 five-minute shows before I left the country. When we got back, no one knew that I had left the country. I also did this show during the football season. I came on and talked about what the Dolphins had done that day in practice. But I wasn't the only one on the radio; several of the other players also had their own shows.

Ted Lampides, a graduate student in music from the University of Miami, wrote a song and asked me to record it after we won our first Super Bowl. It was about the Super Bowl and the pass, and it was to be named "Yepremian's Lament." It was a cute song and had Middle Eastern music in the background. I recorded it during the 1973 training camp, along with a Greek and English song for the flip side of the 45. We were done in two hours. It sold about 5,000 copies and was played on national TV by Howard Cosell.

I was on the television show *Life's Most Embarrassing Moments*, hosted by John Ritter, with Jim Marshall of the Minnesota Vikings. He was famous for intercepting a pass, running the wrong way and thinking he had scored a touchdown when he actually ran into his own end zone, causing a safety for the other team. He was actually one of the best defensive linemen of his time, though.

The program format included showing a film clip, and then the person got up and described what happened. Basically, Jim and I thought, do we have to see this again? We had seen these plays enough. We got paid, not much, but we laughed about it because it was publicity and got our names out there.

I also did the *Today Show*, and Phyllis George interviewed me in the Orange Bowl. She had a cup of orange juice in her hand when a strong wind came along and knocked it all over her dress. Dick Schaap had me on his show after I broke the record for the most consecutive field goals. I was also on Bob Hope's show, the *Mike Douglas Show*, *The Odd Couple*, and did my own show, *The Live Show*, on WGAL in Lancaster. I also did several TV commercials and am a member of the Screen Actors Guild.

The Dolphins made a recording of Christmas songs in 1971. They took all of us to a recording studio, and six or eight players did solos. Unfortunately, the album didn't sell.

I hated to fly. To ignore my fear, I played blackjack in the back of the plane. On every flight, the players would break all of the seats in the back row of the plane so that they could sit backwards and face each other to play cards.

The pilot would always announce, "We are taking off. The Casino is open in the back. Garo is waiting to deal. Players that want to play, go to the back."

I dealt because I was the one that would take a chance. If you are dealing the cards, the percentage is good that you will win. Even if the dealer loses, but plays long enough, he'll eventually win. I told the players if they got blackjack, I would pay them double, and they would have the privilege of dealing. If they didn't want to deal, I would pay them $20 and buy the deal right back.

In addition to the players, some car dealers would come with us on the flight and join us in the card games. That way, they could say they played cards with the athletes.

After we landed, the writers would always ask if I won. When I told them that I had, they said, "It is a lock. You will win the game tomorrow." This happened in every game during the perfect season.

In 1970, Doug Swift and I decided to live together. His girlfriend, Julie, whom he would later marry, came down and helped us look for an apartment. Julie did a lot of research and found us a nice place to live. We decided to check it out ourselves to find out how much it cost. We got in his car, an old Dodge convertible with a busted exhaust pipe, and headed to Miami Beach.

We saw this beautiful high-rise by the ocean that must have been 40 or 50 stories tall. Here we are, two young guys, with Doug in his shower shoes, cutoff shorts and a sleeveless T-shirt. We went in the lobby, and it had nothing but brass and gold. I thought, "What are we doing here?" They took us to the sales office on the 40th floor.

I thought this would cost a lot of money that we couldn't afford, and the guy said that because we played for the Miami Dolphins, they would give us a good price. It was a two-bedroom apartment with a balcony on the front. The rent was $2,800 a month, but he would give it to us for $1,800 a month. I was making $300 a week at that point, and there was no way I could pay for it.

We left and found an apartment near the airport for a decent price. It had two bedrooms—one with a king-size bed and the other with two beds. We flipped a coin for the rooms; Doug won and took the room with the two beds. I couldn't believe my luck.

We were like the odd couple. My side of the apartment looked great, because I was perfectly neat, and Doug's side was a major mess. We lived together that year and had a lot of fun, in spite of living habits.

The trainers had this spray that would cool an injury, like when somebody twisted an ankle. It was like ice, and it gave relief.

Once I went to the trainer's table, picked up one of those bottles, and wrapped it in a towel with the nozzle open. Everybody was sitting in the locker room reading newspapers, so I walked by and squirted people from behind. They thought the air conditioner was leaking. They got up and checked to see where the leak was coming from, then went back and sat down. I'd go back and squirt them again. I fooled them for a while by using it on different guys.

Later on, another player got the same idea. Next thing you know, the trainer ran out of those bottles. He was spending more money on that solution then anything, because everybody picked up a bottle and we were having wars in the locker room.

They put an end to that by saying that nobody would use those bottles again.

Coach Shula or Carl Taseff would check our rooms for the 11 p.m. bed check in training camp and at the hotel the night before the game. (We stayed in a hotel before every game–home or away.) Shula was very clever. He knew that if we went to a strange town like Los Angeles or New York, there were a lot of diversions to get us in trouble.

At night, we were free around 6:30, but at 9 p.m., Shula had a snack meeting. We would have beer, hamburgers, and chips, and Shula did that on purpose because he wanted everybody at that meeting. We only stayed for about 15 minutes, with the coaches talking about the next day for five minutes or so. This way, Shula would keep guys in the hotel. If we didn't have that 9 p.m. snack, guys would go out to dinner or parties and come back at 11 and be tired. This was the best way to manage the players.

The guys on the team who were cheapskates and didn't want to spend money for dinner would wait for the meeting to eat. We still had stragglers come in, but it was very unusual. Football players are people who can eat.

We had a car dealer who loaned cars to the coaches and the organization. Some of them went on road trips with us. One time in 1977, we had a game in Buffalo and had two people from a Chrysler dealership with us. One of the guys played cards with us in the back of the plane and was very friendly.

When we got off the plane, he asked me to get seven or eight players together because he wanted to treat them to dinner. I told him seven or eight might be too many because we ate a lot, so he should take only two players besides me. I called Wally Pesuit, a backup center, and Ed Newman, who told me he wanted to wait for the snack. When I told Ed that a car dealer was treating, he was down the three floors to my room before I even hung up the phone.

When we got to the restaurant, we needed jackets. They loaned them to us and mine fitted, but they couldn't find jackets for the other two guys that were big enough. Ed and Wally put on the two biggest jackets they had and still looked like they were wearing bibs.

Those two guys ate enough for 10 people, ordering six shrimp cocktails just for starters. The dealer was so excited seeing them eat that he told them to order more. There were five of us–three athletes and the two Chrysler guys–and the bill was $580 plus tip.

The next day the dealer told me it was a good thing that I told him not to invite eight players.

Chapter 7

Teammates, Friends and Acquaintances

Larry Little was a big man, but he was the fastest lineman in the league. He was in his prime when we played together. When we played our season opener on AstroTurf in Kansas City's new stadium, it was a hot muggy day. It was 98 degrees and 120 on the field, and when we came back off the field, we would put our feet in buckets of water to cool them off. When we went back on the field, you could hear the feet squashing away.

Larry tried to psyche us into not letting the heat bother us and show the other team we were fresh and ready to play. Little was about 265 then, but he had a certain aura about him. When opponents saw him coming towards them, deck them at full speed, then get up and tackle somebody else, they knew this guy meant business. Larry, Bob Griese, and Larry Csonka were our offensive captains.

Larry Little was a bulwark of the offensive line.

Larry had a distinctive voice. If I was in the locker room or shower, I would imitate him, and people thought he was there. One day he heard about me imitating him. As I was walking out of the shower, he was waiting for me. He grabbed me by the neck and said, "Hey, little man. I heard you have been doing me." I turned around and said in his voice, "Larry, would I do such a thing?" Larry broke up laughing. He is one of my best friends. To this day, we see each other three or four times a year.

When he was the football coach at Bethune-Cookman College in Daytona Beach, Florida, it was one of the major football powers. A lot of great football players came out of there. We had a roast for him, with Howard Cosell as emcee. Two teammates, "Mercury" Morris and Manny Fernandez, were part of the program.

When they asked me to get up and talk about him at the roast, nobody knew about my ability to imitate him. I went to the podium and used his voice to make my speech. He was under the table laughing. When he got up to speak, all he had to do was give me a mean look. He didn't have to say anything. Then he said, "I'll take care of you," with a laugh.

Larry was voted All-Pro honors six times (1971-1975, 1977) and was a Pro Bowl selection four times. He was the first player in the NFL to be named as AFC Offensive Lineman of the Year three straight years (1970-72) by the NFL Players Association. Larry was voted into the Hall of Fame in 1993.

Jim Langer

Jim Langer was voted into the Pro Football Hall of Fame in 1987 in his first year of eligibility. He was a very quite man with a mission. He had the strongest legs and was powerful, quite and unassuming. He was strong-willed, did his job, and never asked for anything. He was very happy with what he was doing and was very content.

He came from the small town of Little Falls, Minnesota, and he still lives there. The Dolphins picked him up off waivers from Cleveland in 1970. He became our starting center in 1972 and played every offensive play that year. When he anchored the line, nobody came through. At the time, Jim and Mike Webster from the Pittsburgh Steelers were the best centers in the league. Jim still holds the club record for the most consecutive games played at 128. A knee injury in 1979 ended his streak. He was All-Pro from 1973-77 and made the Pro Bowl six times, five as a starter.

Bob Kuechenberg was a great offensive guard, but he was overshadowed by Larry Little, a future Hall of Famer. Bob was drafted by the Philadelphia Eagles

*Former Miami Dolphins head coach Don Shula cel-
ebrates with teammates of the 1972 Miami Dolphins
"perfect season" team as they were honored during
halftime of the Miami Dolphins Buffalo Bills game at
Pro Player Stadium in Miami Monday, Nov. 17,
1997. At left is the widow of Maulty Moore. (AP
Photo/Hans Deryk)*

in 1969. Later that year, he played with the Chicago Owls in the Continental League before coming to Miami in 1970.

When Miami joined the American Football League in 1966, Norm Evans was taken from Houston in the expansion draft. He was a starter from the beginning. Norm was the spiritual leader of the team. He is a minister now and runs Pro Athletes Outreach from Seattle, Washington. He was a great lineman and a great family man. He was never heralded and didn't get the publicity. Norm was one of those unsung heroes.

Doug Crusan was our left tackle and the comedian of the team. He used to put on the rookie show every year during training camp, and he gave himself "the honor" of choosing the ugliest guy on the team. I won't name the people that he picked, but it wasn't me. I didn't make the grade. I must have been below ugly. He was always cheerful and funny. He laughed at all times. Doug enjoyed every minute of pro football.

Norm Evans, now a minister, was an unsung hero of the Dolphins.

Wayne Moore was an offensive tackle and played more as a starter in 1972 than any other time up to that point. He was the gentlest giant I ever saw. Wayne lived in our neighborhood, and once we were on stage at the elementary school for our children's career day. Sadly, he passed away too soon.

Larry Csonka was so big and strong that if somebody was in his way, he wasn't quick enough to give that stutter step; he gave an elbow. His forearm was like a baseball bat. Larry would hit somebody in the face, knock him down and run through him. Larry was tall, and his legs were big. It was difficult for a defensive back to knock him down, because Larry was about 250 and built like a bull. He wasn't afraid of anything.

If he had a broken nose, he would still run over people. Larry would have broken ribs and still play. He was that type of a player, a type that I had never seen before. He worked very hard and never took a day off from practice. He was the toughest guy I have ever seen as a running back. Larry was a true fullback, the best I ever saw.

Larry Csonka

He was inducted into the Pro Football Hall of Fame in 1987, his second year of eligibility, along with Jim Langer. Today, Larry lives in Ohio and has a home in Florida. He is a motivational speaker.

J im Kiick was a good blocker and a perfect back on third down, where they would fake the run and pass the ball to get the first down. Jim would run the out pattern. He was always good with his hands and had quick moves, and he would get that eight to ten yards needed to bail us out of the hole. Jim was a great running back and could run through the line, but he was also an excellent pass receiver.

Jim scored the winning touchdowns in our three 1972 playoff games. He didn't have a nickname like Reggie Jackson, "Mr. October," but he was our "Mr. Steady." He was always ready to play, and Shula knew when to switch him and "Mercury" Morris. You could always count on Jim Kiick to get a first down when you needed one. Jim lives in Florida and works for the casinos.

Jim Kiick, running back, breaks into the open field.

When we took out Jim Kiick, we would bring in "Mercury" Morris, who had speed. Csonka would be hitting pass after pass and getting the yardage. Then we'd put in Mercury, and he was gone. The other team's defense was off balance when we changed from Mercury to Kiick with Csonka still running the ball.

Csonka ran for 1,117 yards, and Mercury rushed for 1,000 yards. That was the first time two running backs on the same team rushed for 1,000 or more yards in the same season. Mercury set our club record at the time with the most touchdowns scored in a season, with 12.

Mercury lives in Florida and does promotional work.

Paul Warfield was one of the most important players that Don Shula brought to Miami. Our running attack was great, but we didn't have any breakaway wide receivers. We had Howard Twilley on one side, a great receiver and a clutch receiver, but he didn't have the burning speed that we needed.

When we made a trade with Cleveland to get Paul Warfield, he was the best pass receiver in the NFL. He could

Mercury Morris

run a pattern and end up at a spot eight different ways. The defensive back never knew what the end result would be. He fooled everybody with his precise running, and when the ball was thrown to him, he never dropped it. Paul was always at the right spot at the right time, and his timing with Griese was very important. Warfield studied the game, was always prepared and never ran the wrong pattern. If the ball was thrown his way, it was either caught or wasn't thrown right. He was a winner and very classy.

Our offense was built mostly around running, but having Warfield there was tremendous, because other teams would say they had to shut down the Dolphins' running game. If they shut down the running game, the passing game would open up. If they started to double-team Paul, which they did, then Howard Twilley would be open or tight ends Marv Fleming and Bill Mandich would be open. Both made clutch receptions in the end zone.

If we had had a quarterback like Dan Marino, Paul would have been catching 120 passes a year, but we were happy the way things were. Paul was the first Dolphins player to be inducted into the Pro Football Hall of Fame in 1983.

Howard Twilley started with the Dolphins in 1966. Howard wasn't the biggest, strongest or fastest receiver. All he did was catch footballs. He would run precise patterns, and when he got there, the ball would be in his hands. I don't remember him dropping any im-

Paul Warfield catches a pass and with his breakaway speed bolts down the field.

portant passes. Howard was dependable, hard working and a winner. Bob Griese liked him. They called him Bob's son because Howard would follow him everywhere. He would be in his shadows on and off the field. He had a high regard for Bob.

Bob Griese was a great quarterback. He was accurate, clever, sharp and called his own plays. He knew that if the running game was going, to mix in something else just to keep the defense off balance and then capitalize on the result. He was a genius at play calling. Bob was one of the nicest people you would ever want to meet. It took a long time to get to know him, but once you did, he was your friend. He had a good sense of humor.

Bob was voted into the Pro Football Hall of Fame in 1990. He lives in Coral Gables, Florida, works in real estate and does college football games for ABC. His son Brian is playing for the Denver Broncos.

Marv Fleming was a great blocker and a great tight end. We almost had six linemen instead

Bob Griese had the brains to be a great quarterback.

of five when Marv was in there. He has four Super Bowl rings, two with Green Bay and two with Miami. He played out his option in Green Bay and joined us in 1970. He caught only 13 passes that year and caught five more when we beat Pittsburgh in the 1972 AFC title game.

Once when we were playing in Buffalo, Marv caught a touchdown pass in the third quarter and found a five-dollar bill in the end zone. He looked for more before he came off the field.

After he retired, he went to Los Angeles and two years later came back to Florida. He visited the Dolphins and came into Coach Shula's office with this diamond earring in his ear, a big rock. He said, "Coach Shula, do you notice anything different about me?" Coach looked up and said, "You are missing an earring." People were wearing earrings in California then, but it hadn't been done in Florida yet.

Marv is a tremendous person, very conscientious, very dependable, never cut corners and worked very hard. He is still the same today.

Bill Mandich backed up Marv Fleming but went into the game in passing situations as a tight end. He wasn't known for his blocking, but he was a great receiver. He caught the winning touchdown when we came back to beat the Vikings.

Bill Mandich

People thought Nick Buoniconti would never play in the NFL because he was too small. We got him from the New England Patriots. He came in and was very quick, very sharp, and he could anticipate where the ball was going. He studied the offenses and knew them as well as the other team. Nick studied very hard, and he knew the right plays. He was at the right hole at the right time.

At times, the defense called their own plays. Sometimes the defensive coaches would send in a play using hand signals on whether to play man-to-man or zone. Sometimes, they told the defense to play the 5-3 defense or the 4-3.

Several times, Nick changed plays when the other team lined up in a certain situation. It was up to him to change the play and change the defense. He was like a defensive coach on the field and a great student of the game. Everybody respected him.

We didn't have any superstars on defense. When we played, nobody knew our defensive players. That was why they were called the No-Name Defense.

Nick passed the bar when he retired and became an attorney. He works for HBO doing *Inside the NFL*. Nick's son Marc went to the Citadel, and in his last year in his final game, he made a tackle on the kickoff return. He had his head down, and when he made the tackle, his head snapped and he became a quadriplegic. The only thing he can move is his head. Nick stood by him and fought for him. Marc went to law school and passed the bar. He is a wonderful young man.

Nick Buoniconti

When Nick was inducted into the Pro Football Hall of Fame in 2001, Marc was his presenter. A lot of us went to the ceremony and the party afterwards. If you need any inspiration, all you have to do is look at Nick and Marc Buoniconti, and see a father pulling for his son. When Marc needed his dad the most, Nick was right there.

Bill Stanfill was a lanky, tall guy who was great on the pass rush and was always in the face of the quarterback. He used to have a truck and lived in Georgia. He once said to me, "I can drive from Miami to Georgia without making a stop." I didn't believe him, because for starters, he would run out of gas. He told me he had two gas tanks on his truck.

Then Bill told me that he drank beer during the trip. So why didn't he have to stop to go to the bathroom? He said that the beer went onto the turnpike. How could he do this while driving 65 miles an hour? Bill said, "I have drilled a hole in the floor of my truck. I put a hose on a funnel, and I have a belt hooked to the funnel. It is tied to me and when I am driving, I go to the bathroom." I didn't believe it, but Bill took me to his truck, and sure enough, he had a hole in the floorboard and a hose. I never heard of that before in my life.

Manny Fernandez and Bill Stanfill were the biggest jokers on defense. When I kicked a field-goal and came off the field, I would see Stanfill and Fernandez standing to-

Bill Stanfill eyes the quarterback to anticipate where the play is going.

gether. Usually one of them was mad at me, and the other was smiling. This happened whether I made or missed a field goal. I couldn't figure out what was wrong.

After a few years, I asked them what was going on. They told me they were betting each other five dollars on every field-goal attempt. One pretended to be mad at me because he lost five dollars. I don't know who came out ahead. I still don't know who won the bet on my Super Bowl kick that was blocked. Maybe they didn't bet on that attempt.

Manny Fernandez was the heart of our defensive line. He had a lot of speed, and when we won the Super Bowl, some people thought he should have been the MVP. Manny was in the backfield and made more tackles (11) than anybody. Jake Scott got the MVP award for his two interceptions. Manny was a hard worker.

Bob Heinz was very quiet, a family person who really cared. His locker was next to mine. I got along with him. Nobody knew he was there except the op-

Manny Fernandez

ponent. Bob knew his assignments and his teammates and could play all four positions on the defensive line.

Vern Den Herder came to the Dolphins in 1971 and became a starter in 1972 when Jim Riley needed surgery. He was a very quiet, businesslike person, a family man who was decent. I don't think he even knew a four-letter word. Bob Heinz and Vern were close friends. He led the team with 10 sacks.

Doug Swift was our left-side linebacker and was the most unlikely player to ever play and start every game in the NFL from his rookie year until he retired in 1976. In college, he played at Amherst. Until him, nobody came from Amherst College and played in the NFL. He wasn't drafted. Nobody invited him to come to an NFL camp.

Doug went to Montreal to play in the Canadian League, and they cut him. In 1970, Shula needed a body in camp. He impressed everyone and played in three Super

Bowls in the height of his career. Doug retired on his own terms and became a doctor like both of his parents.

Doug used more tape then anybody on the team. Every toe, finger, hand and ankle had to be taped up. Everybody started following Doug's lead. He knew that on the PolyTurf field that we played on at home, it was very easy for a player to twist an ankle or get turf toe. After a while, the trainer started to complain and wanted to know why everybody was using all his tape. Doug was the most easygoing guy, but he knew what he was doing.

Mike Kolen was the right linebacker. He was called "Captain Crunch," a nickname that he got in college at Auburn because he could hit. Mike wasn't the biggest guy. He weighed 220 pounds.

Dick Anderson was a free safety and didn't have the quickest speed, but he was always in the right spot at the right time. He could return punts and kickoffs and was a great safety. If we needed him to punt, he could do that as well. In the 1971 AFC Championship game, Dick intercepted Johnny Unitas's pass and returned it 62 yards for a touchdown. There were six perfect blocks on the return.

The heart of our defensive backfield was Jake Scott, number 13. He wasn't one of the biggest guys in the world, but he was a great strong safety. He made a lot of interceptions and was a great hitter. Jake could also return punts and kickoffs. He was one of the best at his position through the years, and I am surprised that he hasn't made it to the Hall of Fame.

Curtis Jackson had the biggest Afro on the team. I don't know how he got all that hair in his helmet. It must have cushioned his head nicely. Curtis was very quiet and unassuming. He worked very hard and was a decent guy.

Jake Scott

Lloyd Mumphord played on the opposite side of the field from Curtis Jackson, behind Tim Foley. He played a lot when we went to five defensive backs and played on special teams. He knew the game and didn't have the greatest speed in the world, but he studied very hard and knew everything that was happening. He was a great cover man, was very success-oriented and wanted to win at all times.

Larry Seiple was one of the most gifted athletes on the team. Larry was our punter and a tight end. He wasn't the biggest tight end, and that was one of the reasons he didn't play full-time. Larry could line up as running back, a wide receiver or a tight end. He threw three passes and completed those. He could also be a defensive back and could also play on the special teams. Larry was important to the team. If he got hurt, nobody knew it. He played 11 seasons with the Dolphins.

Alex Karras was a great football player. In my first game, the Lions were losing the game badly when I was asked to kick an extra point. I made the kick and ran to the sidelines cheering. Alex came over and said, "What the *@#$ are you celebrating?" Not knowing much about the game at that point, I turned to him and said, "I keek a touchdown." He took that line and used it on *The Tonight Show* and became a star. To this day, he hasn't paid me a commission for supplying him with such great material.

George Young often scouted the Dolphins' next opponents before he became the general manager of the New York Giants. He would give us a tremendous report on the other team.

Young took care of the special teams when we had our meetings. In 1977, he asked the kickers to fill out a questionnaire. The first question was "How wide is the goal post?" I wrote down, "I don't know. I don't really care. All I know is I kick it through there." I was finished in five minutes.

Everybody else took 45 minutes to answer 20 questions. Those questions weren't going to help me kick better. Young didn't like the way I answered his quiz, telling me that I should have taken it seriously.

The next day, Coach Shula saw me in the hallway and said, "What is this? Can't you take this test like the rest of the players? You wrote in a poem." Shula used to do things as a joke and then walk away. But he made his point. He was saying that what I did wasn't right and the next time I should do what was asked of me.

I met Muhammad Ali in 1967, when I played for Detroit. Roger Brown, a teammate of mine, introduced me. Ali was my favorite fighter. I have seen him at many functions. Ali had a great trainer, Angelo Dundee, and I got to know him as well. Both of them are amazing people.

When I moved to Pennsylvania, I played in Richie Ashburn's golf tournament every year, a tournament that is still successful. I enjoyed listening to him call the Phillies games on radio and television. He was a real nice guy who was loved because he cared for people both young and old. My family and I feel fortunate that we met him.

Yogi Berra is one of the greatest people on earth. He is loveable and sharp. There was an automatic bond between us. He enjoyed meeting Maritza, and we enjoyed meeting his wife, Carmen. We would have breakfast together whenever we were together in a golf tournament. When I go to the Montclair Country Club for a charity tournament, I always introduce myself and say, "Yogi, Garo Yepremian." Yogi says, "I know who you are."

Howard Cosell was one of my favorite people. He was a unique individual, and I thought he was a genius. My family and I would go to the beach in Key Biscayne and stay at a hotel. We'd spend time at the pool so the kids could swim, and Cosell would be there with his grandchildren. Once he asked me to watch them. He was gone for half an hour, and I felt honored that Cosell trusted me with his grandchildren.

When he passed away, I got an invitation to go to his memorial service. Billy Crystal, Muhammad Ali, Joe Frazier, and Lee Roy Nieman were some of the people who attended. There were movie stars, comedians and the Mayor of New York, but only three football players. I felt special to be there. Afterwards, they took us to "The Tavern on the Green," where I spoke with his daughter and offered my condolences. I wondered why I was one of the few football players that was invited. She said, "My dad loved you."

I met Joe DiMaggio in 1992 at a golf tournament for Bryant Gumbel at Disney World. I made one of the biggest mistakes of my life, or should I say, it was Maritza's mistake. She wanted something for the boys and bugged me to get his autograph. I didn't want to bother him, but she finally twisted my arm.

During the cocktail hour, I went over and introduced myself. He was very gracious, and I said that my wife would like to get his autograph for our sons. It was like a curtain coming down; he was immediately a different person. At the time, it bothered me. He said he couldn't do it right away, but would sign something later, because people were watching. I didn't ask him later, but I understood why he didn't sign. DiMaggio had a contractual agreement that he couldn't break.

I met Steve Garvey at a tennis tournament. My sons were with me, and they had a piece of paper and pen ready to get his autograph. Steve said he would sign the papers, but he wanted their address. About three weeks later, they got 12 or 14 baseball cards signed by him. Needless to say, the boys were thrilled. Thanks, Steve.

I never met Wayne Gretsky, but I had dinner in his restaurant with Marv Fleming, Larry Little and Earl Morrall in Toronto. We played in a charity golf tournament benefiting the children's hospital in Toronto. There were ten of us, including our wives, and we all had a delicious meal. The restaurant took care of the bill. They told us it was on Mr. Gretzky. Thank you, Wayne.

I met Michael Jordan at the Jimmy Valvano golf tournament in North Carolina. The night before the tournament, there were more than 1,200 people there for the dinner. Maritza heard this big commotion, and we looked over and saw all these bodyguards around when Michael went to his table. There must have been 100 people trying to see him.

Maritza wanted to go over and talk to him, but I told her enough people were bothering him. Of course, she was persistent, so we went over. He got up from his table and gave me a big hug. I said that I didn't think he would recognize me or know who I was. He said, "I grew up watching you." That made me feel wonderful. We didn't take much of his time.

The next year, I saw Michael coming towards me in the banquet's hallway. Maritza wanted a picture of the two of us. He said, "Let's do it quickly before everybody else shows up." He had his arm on my shoulder and the biggest smile.

I met Harry Kalas at Richie Ashburn's golf tournament. He does a great job announcing the Phillies and highlights for NFL films as well as pro football games on radio. During the cocktail hour, I brought my sons in, and they asked him to autograph a microphone. He picked it up and said, "I have never been asked to sign a microphone before." Harry is my boys' biggest idol. They had pictures of the Phillies all over their walls when they were in college, and both like to imitate him. Harry is a real professional, and I am happy that he was inducted into the Baseball Hall of Fame.

I met Michael Landon when I played tennis at the Jerry Lewis Tennis Tournament for Muscular Dystrophy in Las Vegas. The night before the tournament, Michael was sitting with his wife and daughter, and I was sitting at a different table with Maritza and my brother Berj. Michael leaned over and said, "I took a shower and used my deodorant, but nobody is sitting with us." So we joined him, and he told us joke after joke and story after story, nonstop for the next hour.

At the time, he was starring in *Little House on the Prairie*. Michael wanted me to be a guest on one of the shows and said he would write a part for me. I went back to Miami and put together a video to send to him. Later, Joey Carr, who acted as my agent, and I went to California to see Michael on the set. He assured us he would use me in an upcoming episode soon, but that never happened. I was disappointed that I never got on his show, and years later we were saddened by his death.

I thought John Madden was a great coach, and I also thought he was the biggest grouch in the world. From across the field I thought he was an animal, screaming and waving his arms. But when I played for him in the 1974 Pro Bowl, I got to like John Madden and found out that he was a caring person. He cared about his players, and he turned out to be one of the nicest people I ever met. Never judge a book by its cover.

I met Willie Mays in Atlantic City, where he was hosting a golf tournament. I introduced myself at a casino, and he had the biggest smile on his face. He gave me a big hug and asked if I had any kids. He gave me two autographed pictures, one for each of the boys.

I met Chuck Noll at a couple of banquets. He was quiet and never looked for publicity. As a coach, he got things done and was meticulous in his preparation. He is a lot of fun to be with and is a tremendous person who cares about his family, friends and his community.

One night, I watched a special on television about Jim Otto and how his body had gone through a lot of pain due to playing football. The next day, I was at a gas station in Miami. Jim was putting gas in his car, and we recognized each other. I never saw a guy as beat up as him. He must have had a dozen operations on his knees. Every day must be a painful day for him.

When Maritza and I were dating, she told me she knew a famous football player, Pete Retzlaff of the Philadelphia Eagles. Apparently he came to her school in Philadelphia, Friends Select, and cut the ribbon to mark the start of the May Fair, a springtime festival.

We went to Super Bowl XXI in Pasadena, California, and who comes and sits in front of me but Pete Retzlaff? I tapped him on the shoulder and told him, "My wife has been talking about you for years." He didn't remember the ribbon cutting, but it's funny how kids remember those things. I know that when I go to schools, kids will remember me.

I played in a golf tournament in Blue Bell, Pennsylvania, and Payne Stewart played two holes with five other golfers and me. I was in awe of the way he hit the ball. He was dressed in aqua pants that came to his knees, with white socks. He was classy, genuine and very nice to the five hackers with him. Payne took his time and made sure that everybody hit the ball. He was very patient with us, and I appreciated that.

When we heard his plane crashed, my son Azad asked me not to fly in any more small planes, just in case.

Dick Vermeil was another coach that I thought I would never want to meet. All I saw was this guy from the other sideline who looked tough and mean. He was always waving his arms and screaming at his players and officials.

Years later, I moved to Pennsylvania. Bill Bergey, former middle linebacker for the Eagles, had once told me to call him if I was ever in Philadelphia. Not long after I moved, I was driving to the airport and got messed up with my directions. I stopped at a gas station. I saw this big guy pumping gas, and I said, "Excuse me." It was Bill Bergey. He gave me directions, and we exchanged phone numbers.

A week later, Bill called and invited Maritza and me over to his house for dinner. Two other Eagles were there, Keith Krepfle and Frank LeMaster, as well as their wives. I thought this was going to be a boring night because I didn't know anything about the Eagles. The next people who arrived were Dick Vermeil and his wife. We had a great dinner, and by the fireplace afterwards the war stories came out. I was captivated by Dick and the kind of person he was. He told stories about most of his players and was very positive. We talked until about one in the morning. It was a great night.

Every time Dick has his golf tournament for the Boy Scouts, I play. He is a special person, and I root for him except when his team plays the Dolphins. Once again, don't judge a book by its cover.

I met Ted Williams when I was inducted into the Florida Hall of Fame along with George Steinbrenner. Both were nice to my family. It made me feel good that they were interested in young people. They spent time with us after the ceremony. The next day, Maritza, the boys, Ted and I were flown back to Miami on a private plane. I said to the boys, "Do you realize who this gentleman is? He is the greatest hitter that ever lived." They were too young to appreciate it, but today, they realize it and tell everybody that they were on the same plane as Ted Williams.

I was playing in a major tennis tournament for the Jerry Lewis telethon in Las Vegas back in the '80s. I finished up a set and looked over at the golf course and saw a large crowd watching this young boy hitting the golf ball. I didn't know who he was. I went over and found Tiger Woods, only about six years old and hitting the ball about 100 yards. He was like a machine and turned out to be the greatest golfer of his time, maybe ever. Who knew that some-day I would sit in front of the television and watch this young kid lead the world in golf?

Throughout the years, when I meet people I of-ten introduce myself as Joe Garagiola, and we all have a big laugh. We had the same hairstyle. Finally, I got a chance to meet him at the Bryant Gumbel golf tour-nament at Disney World. We had our picture taken together. Joe wore his glasses, and I wished I had my glasses on when the picture was taken because we would have looked like perfect bookends. He is a nice person and a funny guy.

Art Donovan, former defensive tackle for the Bal-timore Colts and Hall of Famer, is one of the funniest people I have ever met. I did a commercial for *Sports Illustrated* with Art and Larry Csonka. Just looking at him makes me laugh. I gave a speech at the Mayor's Breakfast at the Hall of Fame in 1998, and when I was finished, he put his finger in my face and said, "You. You are good." He started hugging me, and when he hugs you, he can hurt you. There is nobody who doesn't like him, and he likes everybody. He will make you feel comfortable right from the beginning. He is like an old-time comedian. If he didn't play football, he could have had his own TV show.

When I was in Detroit, Dick "Night Train" Lane had just retired and was an assistant coach. He was nice to me and helped me because I didn't know anything about the game. I stayed in touch with him. Several years after I left Detroit, Steve Watson of the Denver Broncos had a golf tournament in Breckenridge, Colorado, and Dick was there.

He was trying to lose some weight and was on a fat-free diet. We stopped at a supermarket and bought enough food for about 10 people, all fat free. He thought he could eat all he wanted as long as it was fat free and still lose weight. A year later on New Year's Eve, I got a call from him. He told me he missed me and Maritza. I felt he was lonely. He had been married to the late Dinah Washington. I saw him a few times after that, but he passed away recently.

Jack Nicklaus called me after we won our first Super Bowl because he had heard that I was an after-dinner speaker. He asked me to speak at his son's school for a father-son dinner. I wasn't a big speaker then, but he knew I was funny because he had seen me on television.

I had a good friend, Dutch Turner, who loved Nicklaus and golf. I wasn't into golf then, but I asked Jack if I could bring Dutch along, and he said that was fine. After my speech, which went well, we got back to Jack's house about 9:30. He had a room with a pool table, and he loved to shoot pool. My friend was a great pool shark from South Philadelphia, although I didn't know that at the time. They played pool, and Jack was really competitive, but Dutch was too good. He knew every trick in the book. Jack was frustrated, but he enjoyed every minute of it.

After three hours of shooting pool, I reminded Jack that he had a tournament starting the next day. He said, "No problem. I'll take my helicopter and be there on time." When we left at 12:30, he gave me a check for the appearance, which I refused to accept.

Two weeks later, he wrote me a note: "Garo, the kids are still talking about your speech. You were tremendous. You didn't take the check that I gave you, so I am having a set of golf clubs made for you, and I will send them to you." A week later, a package came and every thing was there: woods, irons, sand wedge, and putter just for me. I still have the clubs, except the seven-iron, which my brother lost when he borrowed the whole set about five years ago. I learned how to play golf with them. I kept those clubs because of the character of the person who gave them to me. I hold Jack Nicklaus in the highest regard.

Chapter 8

Life After Football

I received more local and national publicity from my playing career when I was cut by the Dolphins than when I made the team. In 1978, I had my best year. I kicked 83 percent of my field goals and made my last 16 in a row, which tied the NFL record. I went to the Pro Bowl in Los Angeles, and after the game, I came back to Miami.

A few weeks later, we had our annual banquet honoring the leaders of the team. They showed a video of the season, and I wasn't even in it. I started thinking about my record-breaking season and making the Pro Bowl and said to my wife, "Something is fishy. I think this past year was my last with the Dolphins." She said that I always said that.

Five months later, we went to training camp, and they had drafted a kicker from Oklahoma, Uwe von Schamann. I was kicking as well or better than he was, but they didn't give me a chance to kick in training camp. After the third exhibition game, I went to Shula and asked why I hadn't had one kick of any kind so far. "If you are not thinking of using me and letting me go, why don't you do it now so I can hook up with another team?" I asked. He said, "Don't you want to play for me?" I said, "You know darn well I want to play for you. I played for you for nine years. I love it here." Shula told me he would see what would happen.

The next week, von Schamann made two field goals, 25 and 26 yards. I felt pretty confident because he hadn't done much. Monday morning, I arrived at the training camp compound to see a note from Coach Shula. This was bad news. When I walked into his office, he looked at me half tearfully and said, "You gave me nine great years. I want to thank you for that, but I have to let you go because we have a young athlete who is coming in as a kicker, and he has a strong leg. We have to go with him and let you go." I turned to him and said, "Thank you for the nine great years that you gave me."

Now the fans were up in arms. They were talking not only about my past kicking, but the various things I did for the community. Reporters were coming up to Shula, and he couldn't give them an answer as to why I was being let go.

I figured it was because of pressure from the owner, Joe Robbie, who had a misunderstanding with my brother Krikor, who worked for Robbie as the general manager of his soccer team, the Fort Lauderdale Strikers. Robbie had the lowest payroll in the league, and Krikor took them to finals, where they lost to the New York Cosmos with Pele for the championship.

Robbie said he was going to give Krikor a two-year contract but never gave him a signed contract. At the end of the year, Krikor said he hadn't received a contract and demanded a contract in writing. Robbie said, "My word is good enough for you." This went on back and forth. Krikor said he was thinking of quitting, and Robbie said that he was thinking of firing him anyway. Krikor left and went to

New York and joined the Cosmos in 1978 as the vice president and general manager.

So Robbie must have been retaliating. Shula might have been pushed to cut me. I can't prove it, though. There is not enough evidence.

After I was cut, I sat at home, and no teams called to pick me up. The second week, the Dolphins played Seattle in Miami. My friends, and the press who were in my yard waiting for somebody to call, said they would pray for me. Nobody called.

My friends convinced me to go to the home opener, even though I didn't want to go. On Sunday, a limo picked Maritza and me up. I put on a fisherman's hat with dark glasses so people wouldn't recognize me. We sat on the 45-yard line in the upper deck across from the Dolphins bench. There was no way they could see me with 80,000 fans in the stadium.

Bob Rubin, a writer from the *Miami Herald*, came over and asked if he could sit with me on the aisle to observe my reactions during the game. I told him it was fine. I don't know how he found out I was there. The game started and he told me to wait for the surprise during the game. I didn't know what he meant.

Von Schamann missed a field goal, and all of a sudden, a huge banner comes out in the stands and it says, "Garo." Two guys were carrying it. My friend said to me, "That's my surprise. I paid those two guys to carry that banner." I told them, "This is terrible." All of a sudden, some people were chanting "Garo, Garo."

Then, in the second half, von Schamann missed an extra point. Not only was that one banner out, but about four other "Garo" banners came out in the crowd. My friend said, "I paid for one banner. Four others must have had the same idea." There were five banners going around the stadium, and 80,000 people stood up and chanted, "Garo, Garo." There was a time-out on the field. Everybody looked for me, including the Seattle players who stood up in front of their bench and turned around. It was unbelievable and surreal for about five minutes. The sound was deafening, and I was embarrassed.

The next night, on *Monday Night Football*, Howard Cosell was giving highlights at halftime and mentioned the Miami-Seattle game. What does he show instead of the game? A clip of me in the stands. Cosell said, "Who is sitting in the stands? The little old tie-maker and tie-breaker, Garo Yepremian. What is he doing in the stands? He should be playing for an NFL team."

The next day, I got a call from the Saints. Their kicker got hurt, and I flew to New Orleans to play for them for the rest of the season. I made four straight field goals with New Orleans to run my streak to 20. My attempt at 21 was blocked; then I made seven straight after that. I was hoping to set that record with the Dolphins.

Even now, when somebody asks me about my football career, the Miami Dolphins are my favorite team. Once you are there for nine years and care about that team, you always regard yourself as a Miami Dolphins player. Had they said, "Why don't you retire as a Dolphins player?" I would have done it. But they didn't.

Coach Shula has always been nice to me, but we never discussed why I was released. He has never said that if he had to do it all over again, he would have kept me. Someday, I am going to force him to say it. Maybe I will grab him by the neck and tell him to say it. About a year ago at a golf course, he came by and said hello. I told the people there, "This is Don Shula, a great coach who made only one mistake in his whole career." They wanted to know what it was, and I said, "He cut me." Shula just looked at me and didn't say anything.

In my book, Shula is the greatest coach I have ever seen. Vince Lombardi was a great coach, but I never played for him. Shula was prepared, he was immaculate and never strayed from his plan. He always went with his instincts. He was prepared thoroughly for anything that would happen. He was tremendous, is a great person, and I'll always look up to him.

Debby Lu is a beautiful girl with a beautiful heart. She met my son Azad at our church's youth group in the autumn of 1994 when they were seniors in high school. They went to each other's proms. Azad went to Millersville University and lived on campus in Lancaster County, Pennsylvania. Debby Lu went to West Chester University in West Chester, Pennsylvania and lived at home. They kept on dating in college even though they were 90 minutes apart.

Four years after they met, they visited us, and we noticed Debby Lu was wearing glasses. She was getting headaches, but she didn't think the glasses helped. She also went to a chiropractor for neck aches and headaches. Her parents thought they were due to carrying her heavy backpack filled with books. When she left, I noticed she was limping and asked if she was hurt.

Debby Lu went for a complete checkup and was diagnosed with an inoperable brain tumor in October 1998. It is called an intrinsic brain-stem glioma. The doctors said that if she took radiation and chemotherapy, she had a 50 percent chance of living five years. Most people with this die earlier.

Azad was very much in love with Debby Lu and told us he was going to marry her sooner or later, but now it would be sooner. He wanted to make her as happy as possible and help her fight this disease. They became engaged at Christmas in 1998.

As parents, you have to guide your children. Maritza and I talked about the good, the bad and the ugly. There would be good days, bad days and a lot of problems. It is great for Azad to be a hero and marry Debby Lu and fight this illness with her. Maybe they would save her life.

I didn't know how strong my son was to do this. He said everything was taken care of, and he had thought this out and wanted to make her happy. We gave him our blessing, and Azad went to her parents and asked for her hand in marriage. They were amazed, shocked, excited and at the same time, were in disbelief. They were happy that he wanted to make that commitment. Her parents told Azad they would help all they could.

With all her problems, Debby Lu graduated in 1999 Cum Laude with a bachelor's degree in psychology, was named the Psychology Student of the Year, and won the Swope Scholarship. Azad graduated at the same time with a double major in business management and economics and a scholarship in football. They were married on November 20, 1999.

Azad works as a commercial morgage loan officer at a bank in their town. After they get up in the morning, he goes to work, then comes home and has lunch with Debby Lu and makes sure she is fine. After lunch, he goes back to work and comes home for dinner. They have stayed away from radiation and chemotherapy and are going with more natural treatments for a while. They are winning the war. But I think it is a steady situation where some days are worse then others. At night, he takes her for treatments in Philadelphia or New Jersey.

They sometimes go to faith healers. They believe in prayer. They are fighting the brain tumor, and financially, it is draining, but that is the least of our problems.

There are a lot of wonderful people in the community, and they are trying to help. Her parents, Harry and Debbie Tashjian, and other relatives have helped. Azad is a warrior. Every time her parents see me, they said, "You don't know what kind of a son you have." I said, "I know. My wife did a very nice job bringing him up and giving him character." Her parents added, "He not only has character, but he is an angel. He takes care of this girl like nobody else could."

Azad never complains and never tells us when there are bad days and he has rushed Debby Lu to the emergency ward in the middle of the night for serious complications. We find out about this later because he doesn't want to worry anybody. Azad has more character and strength then anybody I have ever seen.

When it comes to the greatest athlete and the greatest caring person in the world, I can never look at anybody but Azad. My son is a 100 percenter at work and at home. He does more than what is asked. He wants to win not only at work but also in life to make sure that his wife survives this and gets better.

My daughter-in-law is losing some of her capacities for walking and her movement, but this girl is a jewel. She never complains through all the pain and treatments. Debby Lu is worth every minute that Azad has given of himself. They are in the fight of their lives, and he is there for her at all times.

He checks on the Internet to see if there are any studies being done on this type of brain tumor and if there is a chance that a new treatment or even a cure might come up. In the beginning, they said there was no cure and they couldn't operate. Azad hopes his wife will be able to stay strong and healthy, because if a cure comes out, he will get her that treatment.

This affects our whole family, including her parents and brother, who have pain but don't show it. They are strong people. It really affects my older son, Garo Jr. When Azad said he was getting married, his older brother said that he could count on him as a brother who would be there for him at all times. Garo Jr. is married to Becky, who made the same commitment, and it has changed our lives.

When you have a son who is married, you like to go see the couple whenever you want to because those visits mean a lot. But it is difficult for Azad to be with us. When Maritza and I want to visit, it has to be at a certain time on a certain day when Debby Lu is feeling halfway decent. We can't stay long because we don't want her to get tired.

For Debby Lu and Azad to have a family is out of the question right now. Grandchildren are on hold, but we have to give thanks because we have a gift that we thought we never had. We knew we had two special sons, but we found out that Azad is more special then we ever thought anybody could be. He doesn't talk about this. When he reads what I've said, he may disapprove that I said so many things about him. He doesn't want to be praised and bragged upon.

Whenever they ask him at work about his wife, Azad just says she is okay and won't give any details. He doesn't want to burden them with his problems. I have seen people who have a toothache and the whole neighborhood knows about it. I had an MRI, and I was screaming the whole time. Debby Lu has gone through MRIs and treatments once or twice a month for more than three years. Azad just hopes he can take care of her and keep her in good shape because if there is a cure, they will be in there, trying their best to beat this disease.

Maritza and I, Garo Jr., and Becky have put our efforts together to form The Garo Yepremian Foundation. The foundation will help with Debby Lu's medical expenses and others who find themselves in the same position. The foundation will also assist medical research for brain tumors and catastrophic illness.

After I retired from football, I worked anything and everything that I could find: advertising, promotional work and sales. I did a lot of commercials and endorsed a lot of products. Most of them didn't work. I owned a used car lot that also had a paint and body shop in Hollywood, Florida. My cousin Varouj has it now. He sold the auto sales but kept the rest of the business. (It is still called Number 1 Paint and Body.) Then I did advertising sales in Florida.

When we found out Maritza had breast cancer and my mother-in-law had Alzheimer's disease, Maritza wanted to move back to Pennsylvania. We moved to Oxford in January of 1991. I moved from a big area around Miami to a little town of about 3,500 people. I had a beautiful home with three acres. There was privacy all around. I felt a little depressed.

When I got up in the morning, I said to myself, "It was good I moved here. Now, what am I going to do?" There were no businesses or major companies around. I thought I made a mistake. I sat under a big oak tree with my coffee and worried. Maritza was worried that something was wrong with me.

I started cutting trees, mowing the grass in the back yard, painting and tearing down walls. Maritza said, "There are just so many walls that you can paint."

The only one thing that I could do that would make me happy was work for a television station. I went to Lancaster, which was about 30 miles away. I went to the station affiliated with NBC (WGAL-TV) and saw the program director. He knew all about me. We talked about football and about other people that I had met in the TV world. He asked me what I wanted to do. I told him that I had been interviewed hundreds of times, so I wanted to do features on the Eagles, the Orioles and Phillies. The program director told me he had three sportscasters and didn't need a fourth but said he would keep me in mind.

After three months, I was ready to give up on that station when I got a call to do a talk show. One of the hosts was leaving to go to Washington, D.C. They asked me to audition on Friday. That same day, my dad was brought home from the hospital after a severe heart attack. He stayed with my brother Krikor, who lived two blocks away. That evening, my father passed away surrounded by his loving family.

I went to the station Saturday and got the job. They asked me to stay for about 30 minutes to work on things for Monday's show. I told them I had to leave, but they wanted me to stay. I said, "I have something more important to do. My father passed away yesterday." They said, "You came in for this interview today?" I said, "I want to get this job. I was trying to do something extra to get it."

I worked on the talk show for three months and found out it wasn't for me. I had to leave at 7 a.m. and be at the station by 8 a.m. Before the show, we had an hour meeting. After that, I had to put on makeup. By 9:30, we talked with our guests, and about 10 minutes before we went on the air, we went out and mingled with the audience.

After the show, I did promos for the following day. After lunch, I came back and lined up future guests. I stayed at the station until about six and got home an hour later. At night, I had to study for the show for the next day. In the meantime, I was invited to banquets and to give speeches, but I couldn't go to those anymore.

After three months, the station called me in and reviewed my performance, good and negative. I told them I was quitting because I didn't want to work 12 hours a day. I wanted to be able to go to banquets and give speeches. They asked me to stay for a month until they could find a replacement.

They didn't want me to leave, and I asked them to let me do football predictions. I came in and taped on Thursday afternoons for the news shows. I was done in five minutes and made more money doing that then I did the talk show five days a week. So I went back to my speaking engagements.

At one of them, I met Dan Boyle, who came from a poor family in the coal-mining region of Tamaqua, Pennsylvania. He built up a furniture business and had 48 employees. Boyle wanted to give something back to the community. He wanted to go to the schools and talk to the students but thought, "Who will listen to Dan Boyle?" He felt he could not work with most ex-athletes, but he could work with me. We had a talk and our ideas clicked. I love kids and like to motivate them to do the right things, such as being honorable, telling the truth and taking care of your family. Ten years ago, we started out doing 12 schools a year and then 20. I still do these appearances.

In between, other people hired me. I gave a speech for Uni-Mart Convenience Stores at their convention, and the CEO came to me afterwards and told me he enjoyed my speech and wanted kids to hear this. I signed a contract with them. I worked with Uni-Mart for five years, doing 50 schools a year.

Basically, what I do now is give motivational speeches. I work for the top speakers' bureaus in the country: Washington Speakers Bureau, Barber and Associates, Sports Stars U.S.A., and Harry Walker Speakers Agency among others. My speeches have always been about love of family, teamwork, having a positive attitude, commitment and a love of this wonderful country.

Once I was on *The Odd Couple* with Jack Klugman and Tony Randall. Penny Marshall was in the episode, and I played Penny's blind date. The episode was called "The Rain In Spain." They flew me to California, and I was there for a week. Maritza was confined to bed at home due to her pregnancy with Garo Jr. and could not travel. Every time they introduced me, I was supposed to be a football player that couldn't speak English. I would raise my arms up like a referee does when he signals touchdown. I would also be doing a kicking motion and saying, "Keek."

They asked me how I was doing. I said "Keek." They asked me about 10 questions and all I said was "Keek."

Penny was very nice to me and said that if I was back in California to please call her. The next time I was in California, my friend Joey Carr was with me. I called her office, and they told us to come to the set where she was taping *Laverne and Shirley*. Penny was back in her trailer resting, and there was a sign on the door, "Do not disturb."

Joey Carr didn't just knock. He banged on the door so hard that Penny stuck her head out the window and was very mad that she was being disturbed from her rest. Then she saw me and came over and gave me the biggest hug. We watched her tape the show. Eddie Mekka, who played Carmine Ragusa in the show, is Armenian. He came over and talked when he didn't have to do any shooting. It was a great experience.

I used to hate golf and knew nothing about it. I thought it was crazy behavior for somebody to hit a golf ball and have to go look for it. Then you hit again and go look for it again. This goes on till you put the ball in the hole. This was frustrating for me, and I only played two or three times a year. My friends used to bug me to play when I was in Miami. I thought golf was a crazy way of spending five hours. Any game that took that long to play was a waste of time.

But finally when I moved to Pennsylvania, my brother and nephew asked me to play a round of golf. After I played three times, I was hooked. Now when I see a golf course, my legs start shaking like a dog does when he sees a fire hydrant.

Since then, I average two to three days a week on the golf course when the weather is good. I am involved in golf tournaments that raise money for children's hospitals and tournaments that raise money to fight cancer, especially breast cancer, because my wife had it. I also play in golf tournaments that raise money to fight Alzheimer's disease.

After a while, Maritza wondered when I was going to go to work for a living, because all I did was play golf. God had given me this opportunity to play golf, and at the same time, I met a lot of good people. I wasted a lot of time not playing golf all those years. Every time I walk on a golf course, I think God has given me heaven on earth.

Both of my sons went to Oxford High School and Millersville University. Azad loved football and ice hockey but wanted to play baseball badly. In junior high school, he tried out for Little League for the first time. He made the All-Star team. He made his high school team because he could hit, but his one problem was that he was a slow runner. A normal hit for others was an out for Azad. He was a step too slow.

The pitcher was the best player, and when he took the mound, Azad was on first base. When the pitcher didn't pitch, he played first base, and Azad sat on the bench. He didn't have a future in baseball but stayed with the team and pulled for everybody.

One day after his junior year, I told him he was wasting his time in baseball. I knew he enjoyed it, but I told him his future was in football because the genes were there to be a kicker. I worked with him for three months, and he made the varsity football team. Azad was so good that he was chosen All-Second Team Delaware/Chester County. He received offers for partial scholarships from Division II and III colleges, including Millersville University.

He chose Millersville University, and they had a pretty good kicker who was a junior. Azad redshirted and couldn't play in any games in his freshman year. He helped out where he could by holding for the other kicker in practice and kicking with him. The coach was so excited having him. Azad backed up the kicker as a sophomore, and I figured when he was a junior, he would be starting. Instead, they brought a new kid in and promised him the punting and kicking job. I saw things weren't going to work out for my son. I couldn't tell him that, but he realized it and said that he was wasting his time kicking and wanted to study. I agreed with his decision. If he didn't think he was going to make it in the pros, why waste his time?

Garo Jr. only kicked during his high school senior year and didn't play in college. He was accurate but didn't have the long range. Azad could kick the ball over 50 yards, but he wasn't consistent. He was new to the game and needed experience.

He told the coach that he wasn't going to play any more football. The coach told him that he had been a great young man who worked hard and stayed with the program and said Azad could keep his scholarship even though he wasn't going to play.

My sons are proud of me. When we went to the 25th anniversary for the Dolphins undefeated season, they thought I had been a pretty good kicker, but when they heard the accolades that were thrown my way, they realized their dad was better than pretty good. They never took me lightly. They have always treated me great.

At the banquet, they announced "We have the greatest quarterback in attendance" and introduced me. I picked up my napkin, waved it to pretend that I was passing it and threw it backwards. I got 500 people laughing. When Shula saw me doing this with the napkin, he stood up, put his hands on his hips and gave me that look again. Everybody was laughing, and he knew what to do to make them laugh harder.

I did a promotion for Sprint PCS called "Where's Garo" before Super Bowl XXXIII in Miami between Denver and Atlanta. The day before the promotion started, Coach Shula and I had a press conference. After we were introduced, Shula put his arm around my neck and pretended to choke me. They took a picture of us, and Coach Shula was smiling in the camera.

I didn't realize what would happen next. I heard a voice from the past, and it was Mike Bass talking behind the stage saying, "I was the recipient of your pass, and I'll be right there." Mike came out, and we were reunited. It helped the Sprint promotion, and it was good for Mike. He got a nice check.

The whole concept of the promotion was that whoever found me anywhere in South Florida during the 10 days prior to the Super Bowl could enter to win a drawing for free tickets to the Super Bowl. They gave out two tickets a day for eight days at eight different stores prior to the game.

To promote me, Sprint put a half-page color ad of me in the newspaper every day for eight days. One day, the ad showed me in a wedding party. It changed the next day and showed me on the beach with lifeguards and beautiful girls. They ran six other different kinds of ads. I wore a Miami Dolphins uniform with a helmet under my arm. The headline said, "If you can spot Garo Yepremian in this picture, that is how easy it is to win two Super Bowl tickets for this weekend. Come and join us." Then was a listing for the location at the grand opening of a Sprint store.

At those openings, they had a radio station remote, Dolphins cheerleaders and music at the store. They had a life-sized poster of Mike Bass made with a net in his stomach, and we had the backward passing contest. Two hours later, we had the drawing, and 500 to 700 people were entered every night.

There was also a football player manikin there, without a head, wearing a number one jersey. Contestants could stand behind the manikin and place their head in it and take pictures with me standing next to them, and I would sign those pictures. They gave away 10,000 10-minute calling cards with my picture on them. They had 100,000 caps made to resemble my hairstyle and passed them out. People walked around at the Super Bowl and looked like me.

The day before the game, they had a major scavenger hunt in Miami Beach on Lincoln Road in the most famous outdoor mall in South Beach. We had other players at different stations, and people would ask them where I was. When they found me behind the mall, they gave me their card which showed they stopped at all the stations to find me. I would place the card in the drawing box. A winner was then drawn from about 2,000 people, and that person received two tickets to the Super Bowl.

The day after the Super Bowl I picked up the *Miami Herald* and saw a half-page ad which said, "All of us at Sprint PCS would like to thank you for the contributions you made to South Florida through the years. This week, while thousands proved that they could imitate your passing, very few can match your class and dedication."

started making neckties in 1969 after I got out of the army. The Detroit Lions released me, and Errol Mann, who had replaced me, was doing a good job. At the time, it looked like my football career was over. The Lions didn't need me anymore. I couldn't get a job. I didn't have a college degree, much less a high school diploma. I wanted to be a soccer coach but was turned down because I didn't have an education. I tried to get a job with the Ford Motor Company on the assembly line where my brother Krikor worked, but they weren't hiring.

One night, Krikor was supposed to go a party. He went to a department store to buy a necktie and came back empty-handed. A tie cost $12 at a time when a shirt cost only two or three dollars. All of a sudden, we looked at each other and had an idea to make our own neckties. Our mom was a seamstress. She was a magician with a sewing machine.

Krikor went back to the department store and bought a tie. I put a blanket on our ping-pong table, and we tore down the tie to see how it was made. Next, I went to a ladies' fabric store and picked up the wildest-colored fabrics. We started making neckties. We started out slow, but it became easier as we went along. We needed the money, because I had brought my parents over, and they were depending on me financially.

We started to look for buyers. I went to a dry-cleaning store, because I figured that women are their major customers and are buyers of neckties for their husbands. People usually went there once a week to pick up cleaning, and that would be a good location. The first store I went to, I told them I had played for the Lions. I showed them the ties with the labels on the back that read, "Hand-made neckties by Garo Yepremian." I told them I wanted to put out a display of ties in their stores. After one week, I would come back and see how many he sold and leave more ties with him. I also mentioned that if he had alterations to be done, we could take care of that.

After six weeks, we had 60 stores selling the ties. We sold them to the stores for $6 each and they sold them for $12. It cost us $3 to make a tie, so we made $3 on each necktie. Financially we had a nice thing going, but Mom could only make so many in a week. Sometimes it got frustrating. A store 25 miles away would call me, after selling two neckties, and have some work to be picked up. He would have one pair of pants to fix. That cost $1.50. We lost money on that deal, but I had to do it because I made a commitment. We did this for six months in Detroit before I went to Miami.

After I made the Dolphins, they heard I made neckties. The press jumped on the story. They took a picture of me in the Orange Bowl with my arms out and neckties hanging on my arms. The following day, I saw the picture in the paper. I got another idea. I went to Burdines, who had eight department stores in southern Florida. I went straight to the president's office without an appointment. The secretary wouldn't let me see him, but I finally persuaded her. I showed him the picture and said he could capitalize on the neckties. He wanted to know how we could market these neckties. I told him if he would sell the neckties, I would supply two football players at each store on our off day for two hours next to my ties, and they would sign autographs. He could purchase the ties from me for $6 and sell them for $12. He called his buyers, and the next thing I knew, three or four of them came in the room. He told them to buy the ties. They ordered 240 dozen ties. I panicked. I knew my mom could only make two dozen ties a week. I had to find a supplier.

I went to manufacturers, and the only thing they were making were normal ties, something you got in K-Mart for $3. I had to do something different. I finally found Lyons Neck Ware, a warehouse in Pompano Beach, Florida. He was excited I was there, and he had neckties piled up by the thousands. He showed me this one bunch that had wild colors. I liked them and hoped to get a good price. He offered the whole lot to me for two dollars each. I told him I would take them if he put a logo on the back that read, "An Original By Garo Yepremian" and deliver them to my house. He accepted the deal.

I had 680 dozen neckties in my two-and-a-half car garage. It was filled up. With all of the assortments, it looked like a designer's collection. We took the boxes in to the living room and made up eight different batches. Then we had to deliver 30 dozen ties to each of the eight stores in our family car.

The next battle was to get the players to the stores. I told them that I had a job for them on Mondays, from 4 to 6 p.m. or 6 to 8 p.m. signing autographs by the neckties. Football players were only making $10,000 to $12,000 a year then, so the first question they had was, "How much do you pay?" I told them, "I have two plans. The first pays $50. The second is a dozen ties." Football players are geniuses at counting money, and they wanted to know what a necktie cost. When I told them it was $12, they figured that came to $144 in neckties, so they took the ties. I liked that deal. The ties cost me $2 a piece. Twelve ties equals $24.

My brother Krikor quit Ford and came to Florida, and we started working together. He wanted to retail the ties and put them in little shops in the malls. We started making our own designs. The best one was a dolphin jumping over a goal post. After seven years in the tie business, we gave it up. I still see people with those ties today, and they still think I am in the tie business. All of the coaches and players bought them and they became collector's items.

I opened a restaurant called "Garo's Super Burger." It was a fast-food restaurant and made char-broiled hamburgers. Whenever we had a nice day, our young employees called in sick. They went to the beach, and I had to go in and cook. Also, the first year we were there, the city tore up the highway in front of our store to enlarge it, and that was very negative for us, as construction lasted for over six months.

Krikor and my dad put in a lot of time in the restaurant. We decided to sell the place, rather then make it a franchise restaurant and open up three or four others. My hopes were that we would succeed and franchise, but it didn't work out. We broke even for four years before we sold the place.

When I went into the army, they gave us a multiple-choice test. For the first answer, I put down A without looking at the question. Then on the second answer, I put down C, and on the third, another A. I did this all the way to the end of the test. I was done before anybody and wound up being a cook. I loved being a cook and love to cook today.

Right after I came home, I said, "I am cooking Sunday breakfast." I prepared for six people. I made pancakes, and they looked great. Nice and fluffy and golden brown. I put out bacon, and I was proud and excited. My brother took one bite of the pancakes and gave me a sour look. I thought he was kidding and making fun of me. My mom took a bite, and I got the same look. I had used the same amount of baking powder for six that I had used for 400 in the army. None of it was eaten. My mom redid breakfast and I lost my job as the family cook.

The first three years that my mother-in-law was sick with Alzheimer's, we moved her to our house. The scary moment was when our boys got up in the morning and told us that she was in their room at 4 a.m. trying to make their beds while they were sleeping. Taking care of her was a toll on Maritza, who had breast cancer and was going through radiation treatments.

Finally, we were advised to place her in a nursing home where she lived for nine years. This was done reluctantly, and only after we had hired a full-time nurse to watch her at home. I know that if we hadn't done this, my wife would have had a nervous breakdown. There was nothing more we could do for her illness, which lasted 12 years.

My mother-in-law was the most active and clean person I ever saw. She was very knowledgeable in politics and current events. She was also the kindest woman in the world and full of love. Slowly, she started forgetting the day and the date. Then she'd repeat questions. She didn't recognize anybody and wouldn't talk.

She was an Armenian orphan from Marseille, France. My father-in-law was also an Armenian orphan. After coming to Philadelphia in 1920, he went back to Marseille and married my mother-in-law in 1927. They came back to Philadelphia, where with her help and hard work, he built an empire of 75 dry-cleaning stores called Original Rainbow Cleaners & Dyers, Inc.

Bob Griese's wife Judi had breast cancer and died in 1986. Dorothy Shula, Coach Shula's wife, died from it in 1991. Maritza got it in 1989 on the left breast. She got a lumpectomy. Fortunately, when they took the lymph nodes out of the breast where the cancer was growing, they found out that the cancer hadn't spread.

We found it at an early stage. That is why it is important for a woman to get regular check-ups. The cure is there if you get it early.

Maritza went through the operation and followed up with 31 days of radiation. She got a clean bill of health after that.

All three of us had good marriages and families. The husbands stood by the wives at all times. When your wife has breast cancer, it affects you, and you feel it is a part of you. It hurts you. This is when you realize that life is important, and your whole attitude towards life changes. You are helpless, because it is not in your hands to cure it. You help them in every way through the pain, not only through the physical pain but the mental pain. When a person has breast cancer, you are right there beside them giving them hope for the future and helping them laugh as much as possible.

Her cancer came back in 1998, in the same part of her left breast. There were calcifications and minor cell changes on the right. The doctor said that he had to remove the left breast because this time the cancer was invasive. The right breast had changes in it that implied that something could happen to the right one as well. He said they could do a lumpectomy on the right breast and a mastectomy on the left one.

Maritza was very tough and very brave. She decided to do the whole thing, have both removed and all the tissues. She fought to save her life.

She had the option of reconstructive surgery, which every woman who goes through a mastectomy should have as far as I am concerned. It is a long process. It is a personal choice. Basically, it is a major ordeal for the woman, but I feel a positive one because her body has changed. She might have trouble with self-esteem. If I had any kind of advice to give, a woman should get reconstructive surgery if she so desires, because it would help her self-esteem, and she would feel much better in many ways.

After playing 15 years, I was released by Tampa Bay and never played again. I still thought I could kick, but I also knew I couldn't do it because I had a pulled left groin on my left leg and a hamstring pull that hadn't healed for three years. I hurt it in Miami, and I nursed it in New Orleans. I couldn't tell the team, because if I did, I would be replaced.

Every morning, I would go to the locker room and get in the whirlpool full of iced water. I would sit down for 10 minutes. The first five, I thought I was going to die because it was so painful. Then I was numbed up. They had a hot whirlpool next to the cold one, and I would get in that. The transition between the two was like needles going through my body. Then I would go to practice. Thankfully, New Orleans and Tampa Bay didn't make me kick very much in practice. They trusted me and knew I was a good kicker.

My mother was the most active person ever and would work till midnight when I was young just to make sure she could give us everything. She was the heart of the family and a big football fan. When she was 53, she was playing tennis every day.

She and my dad, my older brother Krikor and his son Sarko, and my younger brother Berj were living about two blocks away from us. Their house had a pool and a lake behind it. We had dinner with them most every night. She had nothing to worry about and didn't have to go to work anymore.

All of a sudden, she became depressed. She didn't want to do anything or talk to anybody. She gave up on life and was suicidal. In the meantime, Berj graduated from high school and all the colleges were trying to recruit him. They came from all over the country.

We got lucky when a group that included some doctors came from Vanderbilt University to impress my brother. They saw my mom and asked what was wrong. I told them she was depressed. They said that it was major clinical depression and said they knew what should be done. They told us a very effective treatment was electric shock treatment. I got nervous, because when somebody tells you that your mother could be shocked with electricity, you feel like they are going to give her a shock that will electrocute her. I also knew that if it would save my mom's life, we would try anything.

Maritza called the hospital and tried to find out where she could get the shock treatment. Maritza had had a miscarriage about one month earlier, and we were just getting over this. My wife got pregnant again about the time my mom's depression started. Maritza had to drive my mom to the hospital three times a week. Mom would lie down in the back of our Cadillac on the 45-minute trip to and from the hospital. They did four or five treatments. She also went to a psychiatrist who set up the treatments.

In about three months, she became like a new person. She lost memory of that time in her life. She didn't even remember what had happened for three months, including the third Super Bowl, which was played during her treatments. That is normal for those treatments. Today, she is alive and well, thank God.

We lost a baby during the 1973 season. We were playing in Miami, and immediately after the game I was supposed to fly to Maine to be the Grand

Marshall in the Portland Parade on Monday. After the game, my brother told me that he had bad news. He told me that we lost the baby last night. I asked why he hadn't called me, and he said it happened at 3 a.m., and Maritza didn't want to bother me because I was with the team at the hotel and had a game the following day.

I called the hospital and talked to Maritza and told her I would come home and cancel Portland. She said she was fine and told me to go to Maine.

We felt terrible about losing the baby. The doctor suggested that we try to have another baby as soon as possible, and Maritza got pregnant a month later. We went to the Super Bowl for the third time three months later to play Minnesota in Houston. After halftime, I was a bit concerned, because I didn't see Maritza in her seat, so I hoped for the best. I did fine in the game and didn't screw up like I had the year before. After the game, I came off the field and my brother Krikor's face looked pale. I asked him, "What is wrong? Is it the baby?" He told me it was. I asked him if we lost the baby and he said yes. I said, "My God, what have I have done wrong? We lost the first one, and now we have lost a second child."

I panicked, and Pete Rozelle, the commissioner of the NFL, came by. He heard what happened and said he would give me a security person to take me to the hospital to be with Maritza. The driver drove full speed through the crowd. I was nervous because I thought he was going to kill somebody on the way.

When we walked into the hospital and asked what room my wife was in, they told me she checked out. I said, "What do mean that she checked out? I was told she lost the baby." The hospital said she didn't lose the baby, only that she was hemorrhaging. They stopped that, and she wanted to go back to the hotel. The wives and the team were staying in separate hotels, so Krikor went to the team's hotel. I went where the wives stayed, but neither of us could find her.

Finally, I got a call, and they told me she was on the team bus with the other wives and players. I went back to the team hotel, picked her up and carried her up to the room and asked why she went back to the game. It turned out that all the cabs were at the stadium, so. . .Maritza and my brother Berj walked two miles back to the stadium so she wouldn't disappoint me and have another let-down.

ABC, CBS and NBC called the room and asked me to come down to do some interviews, but I told them I was staying in the room with my wife. I had a cousin there who was a doctor, and he assured me Maritza was all right, but I wouldn't leave. I never made it to either victory party.

I had to leave for the Pro Bowl the next day, so my brother flew on the team plane back to Miami with Maritza. Shula had an ambulance waiting at the airport when they arrived. Garo Jr. was born seven months later on July 28, 1974 and weighed eight pounds, seven ounces. I went to the Pro Bowl and kicked five goals and was voted Most Valuable Player in the game.

My brother Berj was 11 years younger than me. After successfully kicking in high school and making All-State in Florida, he was highly recruited by top colleges, including Vanderbilt, Clemson, Florida State, Florida, George and Alabama. He chose the University of Florida. He broke numerous school records and was named an All-American. He was a great kicker and never missed a field goal inside 40 yards in high school or college.

Upon graduation, he was told by many team represen- tatives that he would be selected very high in the NFL draft. Unfortunately, those were empty promises. He was never drafted and wasn't even invited to an NFL team camp as a free agent. It took $1,000 from me to give an agent to get into the Cleveland Browns training camp where he reinjured his ankle. He never played in the pros.

Coincidentally, this entire episode happened the year my older brother Krikor had parted ways with his employer Joe Robbie, the owner of the Miami Dolphins and the Fort Lauderdale Strikers pro soccer team of which Krikor was the general manger. Ironically, I was cut by the Dolphins after a Pro Bowl season in 1978. How strange is that?

The road to my appearance on a Bob Hope spe- cial started when I was giving a five-minute stand-up comedy routine at the Miami Beach Convention Center for the Firemen's Fund for Firemen. Phil Donohue and Anita Bryant were there, along with some other stars. For me, this was like being in fantasyland, with all of the big names.

I gave my five-minute speech and ran into Bob Hope backstage. He came up and put his arms around me and wanted to know who wrote my jokes. I said "These are things that happened to me." Hope said, "I can't believe this. Somebody is writing your jokes." I said, "No, I do them myself."

He asked me if I would mind doing his show at the Fountainbleu Hotel. I told him I would be glad to. It was a $1,000 per plate dinner for Parkinson's disease. Hope did this every year, and he always brought in a lot of stars. I did this for three or four years. One time, he made me sing. I sang one song, and he wouldn't come out and pick me up. So I had to stay there. I did Ray Charles, Louis Armstrong, Dean Martin and Elvis Presley. Finally after 15 minutes, Hope came out and thanked me. The reason he left me out there so long was he found out that President Ford was at the Eden Rock Hotel next to the Fountainbleu on Miami Beach. He went through their security and got to President Ford and brought him over. It was a big thrill meeting the president.

A few years later, in 1975, Hope asked me to go on his TV show with George Goebel. I stayed at the Sheraton Hotel in Hollywood at the Universal Studios. They told me my script would be delivered to the room. I had to study it, and the following day, they would pick me up at 5:30 and take me to the studio.

The limo came and took me to the studio. I walked in, and the guy asked me if I had my script with me and had I studied it? I said, "What script? Nothing was sent over." He told me that George Goebel also didn't get his, so we saw the music director. He taught us a song that only took us 10 minutes to get down right. They had teleprompters so we wouldn't miss our lines.

I was playing a football player that couldn't speak English, and Goebel was my coach and interpreter. Bob Hope got up and said, "Here is my good friend, George Goebel." He came in, and Hope asked what he had been doing.

Goebel told him that he was a football coach, so he had been traveling all over. "In fact, I have my player," he said. He asked me to come out but gave me a fake name.

I came out wearing a fisherman's hat, and Bob thanked me for being on the show. Goebel asked me a question, not in English but a made-up language, and I answered him back in Armenian. Then Goebel "translated" the response to Bob in English. Bob asked how I started kicking the ball. Goebel "translated," and I said in Armenian, "When I was born, they put a football in my crib and I kicked it and it kept on going. So I continued practicing." This went on for about five minutes, then Bob thanked Goebel and told him to thank me. By the time Goebel turned around to thank me, I turned around and said to Bob Hope, "I have been a big fan of yours. I watch and have a lot of respect for you."

He got on Goebel for fooling him by telling him that I couldn't speak English. Then Hope turned around and said, "Ladies and gentlemen, if you don't know who this is, this is Garo Yepremian of the Miami Dolphins." I took my hat off and bowed, and the music started, and he started singing. Then we sang together. We did it in one take, and it was perfect in front of a live audience.

Bob Matheson was number 53 at linebacker and they called it the 53 defense, because he had the option of lining up as a defensive lineman or linebacker. Later on, Lawrence Taylor did it with the Giants.

In 1978, we went to Philadelphia to play the Eagles. My in-law's wanted to take me out to dinner the night before the game. Bob was there and he came along. A month later Maritza's dad passed away. Bob saw Maritza and told her that he had a great dinner with her parents and had enjoyed meeting her father and how nice he was. It meant a lot to Maritza.

I met my wife Maritza on October 28, 1970. I was signing autographs at the opening of Chicken Unlimited along with Doug Swift, Mercury Morris and Larry Little. Maritza was attending the University of Miami. Some friends told her about me. Maritza was a big soccer fan. She came to the opening and asked me for my autograph and told me that it was for her cousin. A friend of hers asked if she could interview me for the college radio station. I told her that was fine. I asked for her phone number and said to Maritza that I might as well get your phone number. I called her four times the next day before I reached her. We went out that night and the following three nights. On our fourth date, I told her I was going to marry her. Maritza asked me if I knew what I was saying and I told her I did. She said yes.

After Thanksgiving, Maritza's parents came to Miami to meet me and my parents also came to meet Maritza. Everybody was happy that we were getting married. After a big engagement party in January, we got married on June 12, 1971.

Celebrate the Heroes of Florida Sports
in These Other Acclaimed Titles from Sports Publishing!

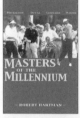